GLOBETROTTER™

Trav

ZAMBIA
AND VICTORIA FALLS

WILLIAM GRAY

NEW
HOLLAND

NEW
HOLLAND

★★★ Highly recommended
★★ Recommended
★ See if you can

Second edition published in 2007
by New Holland Publishers (UK) Ltd
London • Cape Town • Sydney • Auckland
First published in 2003
10 9 8 7 6 5 4 3 2 1

website: www.newhollandpublishers.com

Garfield House, 86 Edgware Road
London W2 2EA, United Kingdom

80 McKenzie Street
Cape Town 8001, South Africa

14 Aquatic Drive, Frenchs Forest,
NSW 2086, Australia

218 Lake Road, Northcote,
Auckland, New Zealand

Distributed in the USA by
The Globe Pequot Press, Connecticut

Although every effort has been made to ensure that
this guide is up to date and current at time of going
to print, the Publisher accepts no responsibility or
liability for any loss, injury or inconvenience incurred
by readers or travellers using this guide.

Keep us Current
Information in travel guides is apt to change, which
is why we regularly update our guides. We'd be
grateful to receive feedback if you've noted something
we should include in our updates. If you have new
information, please share it with us by writing to the
Publishing Manager, Globetrotter, at the office nearest
to you (addresses on this page). The most significant
contribution to each new edition will receive a free
copy of the updated guide.

Publishing Manager: Thea Grobbelaar
DTP Cartographic Manager: Genené Hart
Editors: Nicky Steenkamp, Carla Zietsman,
Melany McCallum
Consultant: Liz Booth
Picture Researcher: Shavonne Govender
Design and DTP: Nicole Bannister, Lellyn Creamer
Cartographers: Elaine Fick, Genené Hart,
Marisa Galloway

Reproduction by Hirt & Carter (Pty) Ltd, Cape Town
Printed and bound by Times Offset (M) Sdn. Bhd.,
Malaysia.

Photographic Credits:
Anthony Bannister: page 115;
Anthony Bannister Photo Library/Philip Berry:
page 9; Anthony Bannister Photo Library/Brendan Ryan:
page 81; Jeff Barbee: page 8; Roger de la Harpe/Africa
Imagery.com: cover; William Gray: pages 4, 10, 12, 13,
42, 45, 49, 51, 64, 66, 83, 84, 90, 114; Dr J. Kloppers:
pages 7, 18, 59, 69, 70; Jason Lourie: pages 20, 36;
Marek Patzer: pages 6, 19, 21, 24, 25, 26, 28, 29, 35,
37, 38, 46, 54, 56, 74, 77, 80, 92, 94, 104, 107, 110,
118, 119; Photo Access Photographic Library/Peter
Blackwell: page 95; Photo Access Photographic
Library/Getaway/ R. Daly: pages 106, 108; David
Rogers: title page, pages 11, 14, 15, 16, 17, 27, 30, 32,
34, 39, 44, 47, 50, 52, 53, 55, 57, 58, 62, 65, 67, 68,
71, 76, 78, 79, 82, 85, 86, 87, 96, 97, 98, 100, 103,
105, 112, 116, 117.

Cover: *Victoria Falls can be admired from a series of
viewpoints.*
Title Page: *A Zambian boy sits outside his colourful
home.*

CONTENTS

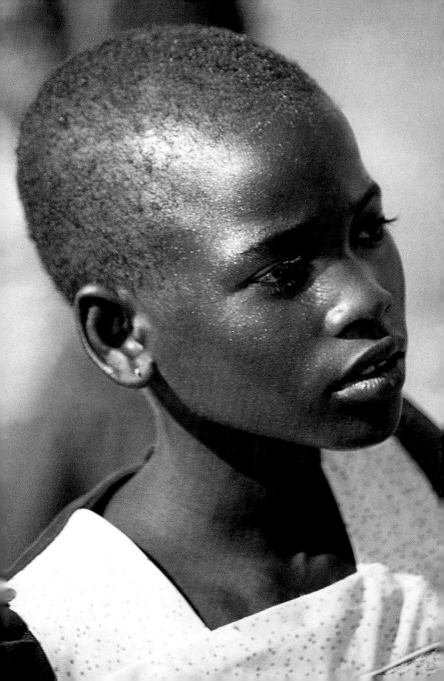

1
Introducing Zambia and Victoria Falls

Vast tracts of wilderness, sensational wildlife and few other tourists. These are the hallmarks of Zambia, a huge landlocked country in the heart of southern Africa. The local tourist board has dubbed this rugged land of plateau, plain, river and swamp 'The Real Africa' – and the moment you set foot in one of its dozen or more national parks, you'll understand why.

Enjoying all the comforts of a classic safari led by expert guides, you can play the explorer in Zambia – whether it's gazing upon the legendary **Victoria Falls** or paddling a dugout through the **Bangweulu Swamps**.

Walking safaris in Zambia provide one of Africa's most thrilling wildlife experiences. Imagine following a game trail in the world-renowned **South Luangwa National Park**, smelling the pepper-sweet tang of the bush, your eyes riveted to the fresh elephant tracks at your feet…

In **Lower Zambezi National Park**, no visit would be complete without canoeing along the river in the company of hippos. The Busanga Plains in **Kafue National Park** is stunning, big-sky country (Zambia's very own Serengeti), while **Liuwa Plain National Park**, far to the west, is home to one of Africa's last great wildebeest migrations.

But Zambia is more than purely a wildlife destination. From modern **Lusaka** and historical **Livingstone** to the traditional Lozi kingdom of **Barotseland** and the extraordinary colonial manor of **Shiwa N'gandu**, Zambia's culture and history are just as fascinating as its big game. At times, 'The Real Africa' can seem anything but real. It is far

TOP ATTRACTIONS

*** Victoria Falls: a natural wonder as well as a centre for adventure activities.
*** South Luangwa walking safari: track wildlife and learn bush-lore in Zambia's premier national park.
*** Canoeing on the Lower Zambezi: a relaxing way to enjoy a beautiful national park.
** Busanga Plains: flood plain in Kafue National Park.
** Shiwa N'gandu: remarkable colonial manor house.
** Nyika Plateau: dramatic highlands, perfect for hiking and horse riding.

Opposite: *Portrait of a Kunda village girl in the Luangwa Valley.*

Above: *Clouds of spray rise from the Victoria Falls, a World Heritage Site on the Zambezi River.*

from any coast, yet boasts sandy beaches where it borders **Lake Tanganyika** – a favourite spot for anglers.

Parks like **Kasanka** and **Nyika** have attractions ranging from boating to hiking and horse riding. **Victoria Falls**, meanwhile, has adrenaline-charged adventures like white-water rafting, abseiling and bungee jumping .

THE LAND

With an area of around 752,617km^2 (290,587 sq miles), Zambia covers just 2.5 per cent of the African continent. It is, nevertheless, a vast country dominated by a great plateau cleaved by two major valleys – the Zambezi and Luangwa. Numerous rivers scratch its surface, oozing across seasonal flood plains or cascading over magnificent waterfalls. Lakes, both man-made and ancient, languish in valleys and depressions, while Zambia's extremes range from high, windswept grassland to hot, sultry swamp.

Highlands and Valleys

Zambia reaches its most lofty in the highlands of the **Nyika Plateau** which rises in the northeast of the country and extends into Malawi. Offering cool respite from the valleys (particularly in the stifling build-up to the rains), Nyika soars to over 2600m (8530ft).

The plateau covering much of the rest of Zambia lies at less than half this altitude. Gently undulating, with only an occasional cluster of hills, it is composed of sediments forged up to 1000 million years ago. These antiquated rocks are a major source of Zambia's wealth – particularly in the mineral-rich **Copperbelt** region stretching northwest from Lusaka.

FACT FILE

Name: Republic of Zambia, formerly Northern Rhodesia.
Independence: 24 October 1964.
Total Area: 752,617km^2 (290,587 sq miles), about three times the size of the UK or twice the size of California.
Capital: Lusaka.
Population: 11.5 million (2006 estimate) with two per cent growth rate per annum.
Time Zone: GMT+2.
International Dialling Code: 260.
Language: officially English, plus over 70 local languages and dialects.
Religion: Christian, Muslim, Hindu and traditional African beliefs.
Currency: Kwacha.
Industry: copper and cobalt mining, hydro-electric power, farming and tourism.

Towards the south of the country and in the far north, the plateau dips abruptly into broad rift valleys hemmed in by spectacular escarpments. Over the aeons, these fractures in the earth's crust have filled with mighty rivers and impressive lakes.

Lakes and Rivers

Although much of **Lake Tanganyika** lies outside Zambia, this 'inland sea' of the Great Rift Valley nicks the country's northern border. After Lake Baikal in Siberia, Tanganyika reaches the greatest depth of any lake at 1433m (4702ft). Like nearby **Lake Mweru**, its waters teem with fish, providing a valuable source of protein for local communities.

A natural template for Zambia's border with Zimbabwe, the **Zambezi River** is Africa's fourth longest at 2650km (1650 miles). Its course from northwest Zambia to the Indian Ocean scrawls a giant question mark across southern Africa, but no one can be left in any doubt as to the beauty and importance of this stately river. From the tempestuous cataracts of **Victoria Falls** to the restrained placidity of **Lake Kariba**, the Zambezi has many moods.

To a large extent, the characters of all Zambia's rivers are influenced by seasonal extremes. Nourished by a vein-like network of tributaries, the **Luangwa River** and **Kafue River** pulse and subside in time to flood and drought. Just as the rivers themselves change throughout the year, so too do the plains and wetlands that surround them.

Swamps and Plains

Every wet season the Zambezi River inundates the **Barotse Flood Plains** of Western Zambia, triggering the annual migration of the Lozi people to higher ground (*see page 117*). The transformation is no less remarkable on the **Kafue Flats** or **Busanga Plains** of the Kafue River

---

TRACING THE ZAMBEZI

Rising in the highlands of eastern Angola and north-western Zambia, the Zambezi has a total length of 2650km (1650 miles), making it Africa's fourth longest river. From its source it flows south across the Barotse Flood Plain, swinging east along Namibia's Caprivi Strip before plunging over Victoria Falls. Downstream of the Falls, the Zambezi enters Lake Kariba and then Cahora Bassa (both created by dams), before spilling its contents into the Indian Ocean near Chinde in Mozambique. The river's catchment area, including major tributaries like the Kafue and Luangwa rivers, is roughly equivalent to the size of Alaska or Australia's Northern Territory.

Below: *Boating and fishing are popular pastimes on Kariba, an artificial lake created in the late 1950s.*

THE MOPANE TREE

Found in many parts of Zambia, the mopane tree (*Colophospermum mopane*) forms extensive woodlands and is easily recognized by its butterfly-shaped leaves. It bears small yellow-green flowers from Dec–Jan and kidney-shaped fruiting pods from Apr–Jun. Elephant, giraffe, buffalo and various antelope relish the leaves and pods, but people also derive a delicacy from the tree in the form of 'mopane worms'. These strikingly patterned red, yellow and white caterpillars are delicious when roasted. Locals avidly harvest them, selling any surplus in local markets.

Opposite: *The dappled shade of a mopane wood provides perfect conditions for a walking safari.*
Below: *A desiccated water hole waits for the first replenishing rains of November.*

where flooded grasslands become inaccessible for half the year – unless you happen to be one of the plethora of water birds or semi-aquatic antelope that thrive in these seasonal wetlands.

Zambia's greatest waterworld, however, sprawls across a shallow basin in the remote northeast. The **Bangweulu Wetlands** combine lake, river, swamp and plain to create a haven for some of the country's rarest wildlife, including the sitatunga antelope and shoebill stork.

Climate

Despite Zambia's location, snug between the Equator and the Tropic of Capricorn, temperatures are largely moderated by the country's altitude. It still has plenty of hot, tropical sunshine, but not the debilitating heat or humidity you have to contend with in the low-lying tropics. There is, however, one notable exception to this. The Zambezi and Luangwa Valleys can become sweltering towards the end of October, with temperatures soaring to over 40°C (104°F) in the build-up to the rains. At the other extreme, occasional light frosts can occur in sheltered valleys during winter.

Zambia has three fairly distinct seasons: **cool and dry** from May to August, **hot and dry** from September to November, and **hot and wet** from December to April. These timings vary slightly depending on where you are. For example, rains often arrive in the north as early as October and may finish in the south by late March.

Rainfall usually reaches its peak in January, and northern areas can receive over twice the annual total further south. Do not, however, be completely dissuaded from travelling during the wet season. The rain can be heavy, but it often occurs as frequent showers interspersed with sunshine. Between February and April, vegetation has been rejuvenated and is wonderfully lush, animals are in prime condition

and the dust has been washed from the air creating good conditions for photography. Access, however, can be a real problem during this so-called 'green season', with only limited activities available, such as river safaris in South Luangwa National Park. Animals can also be more difficult to spot compared to the dry winter months, by which time termites and other herbivores have munched their way through much of the wet season growth.

Plant Life

Zambia's vegetation forms a patchwork of grassland, woodland and swamp. Within these broad categories are numerous distinct plant communities, the most dominant of which is **miombo woodland**. Covering nearly three-quarters of Zambia, this deciduous woodland thrives on the generally poor, acid soils of the plateau. One of its distinctive trees is *Brachystegia* which produces rich, autumnal colours in early spring (September) before the new leaves gradually turn yellow and then green.

Confined mainly to the valleys, **mopane woodland** makes pleasant walking country. Not only does it offer shade, but the leaves and pods of the mopane tree attract browsing animals, such as elephant and giraffe.

Other types of tree communities to be found in Zambia include lush **riverine woodland** – a tangle of wild gardenia, strangler fig, sausage tree, ebony and mahogany often found along watercourses.

Permanent areas of **swamp**, like those found in the Bangweulu Wetlands, run riot with aquatic plants like water lilies, papyrus

CLIMATE

Most people visit Zambia during the dry season from May to November. There is a greater choice of camps, lodges and activities available during this period, and getting around is much easier compared to the wet season. Wildlife also tends to be more easily spotted at this time – the vegetation is less rampant and obscuring, while animals often congregate near shrinking water sources. If you do visit during the middle of the dry season, remember that this is Zambia's winter and it can get very cold at night.

COMPARATIVE CLIMATE CHART	LUSAKA				LIVINGSTONE				MFUWE			
	SUM	AUT	WIN	SPR	SUM	AUT	WIN	SPR	SUM	AUT	WIN	SPR
	JAN	APR	JULY	OCT	JAN	APR	JULY	OCT	JAN	APR	JULY	OCT
MIN TEMP. °C	17	15	10	18	19	15	6	18	20	17	10	19
MAX TEMP. °C	26	26	23	31	30	30	26	34	31	32	29	36
MIN TEMP. °F	63	59	50	64	66	59	43	65	68	63	50	66
MAX TEMP. °F	79	79	73	88	86	86	79	93	88	90	84	97
RAINFALL mm	231	18	0	10	174	24	0	25	190	60	0	19
RAINFALL in	9	1	0	0.5	7	1	0	1	7	2	0	1

Above: *A young lion in South Luangwa National Park seeks shade during the heat of midday.*

grass and phragmites reed. **Flood plains**, on the other hand, have little more than grasses which are able to cope with both the seasonal inundation of water and the intensive grazing pressure of large herds of animals.

The Wildlife

Wildlife is to Zambia what the Opera House is to Sydney, Table Mountain is to Cape Town or the Statue of Liberty is to New York. You simply can't leave without seeing it. Even if you only spend an afternoon on a game drive in Mosi-oa-Tunya National Park near Victoria Falls, you will at least experience some of the suspense, thrill and wonder that is unique to an African safari.

Part of the special appeal of a Zambian safari lies in the variety of wildlife-viewing options (game drives in open vehicles, night drives, walking safaris, canoe trips, etc) and the excellent range of national parks. Very quickly, you will be totting up an impressive list of the more common large mammals and birds – and if you're lucky, one or two rarities.

The Big Five

Lion, leopard, elephant, rhino and buffalo. Everyone hopes to see the 'big five' and in Zambia you stand an excellent chance. Only rhino will elude you, unless you visit Mosi-oa-Tunya National Park where a small group of **white rhino** is protected. Black rhino, eradicated from Zambia by poachers during the 1970s and 1980s (*see* page 14), were reintroduced to North Luangwa National Park in 2003.

The **lion**, Africa's largest predator, is still common throughout Zambia, particularly in the larger national parks. This sociable cat lives in prides dominated by one or two males, but it's the lionesses that do most of the hunting. Lions have been known to kill anything from tortoises to baby elephants. They are most active at night – a time when you are most likely to hear the evocative guttural roar of a lion proclaiming his territory.

The **leopard** is a solitary nocturnal hunter, relying on cover and stealth to ambush prey. South Luangwa National Park, riddled with patchy woodland and twisting waterways, suits this beautiful spotted cat perfectly. Night drives here have become renowned for leopard sightings.

Zambia is a stronghold for the **elephant** with over 15,000 occurring in the Luangwa Valley alone. Lower Zambezi National Park is also an excellent place to observe them. Intelligent and social, elephants form closely bonded herds led by the eldest female or matriarch. Adult males, which can weigh up to 6000kg (13,230lb), form separate bachelor groups.

The **buffalo** is another sociable beast. North Luangwa, in particular, supports large herds of these generally peaceful grazers. Despite being labelled as grumpy and aggressive, it is usually only solitary old bulls that you need to be wary of.

Antelopes

Zambia has a wonderful range of antelopes – due largely to the fact that these elegant creatures have diversified to fill every imaginable habitat. In Zambia, there are two extremes – the amphibious, swamp-dwelling **sitatunga** and the nimble **klipspringer** of rocky slopes. In between are species more associated with woodland and plain.

Two of the most commonly encountered are **impala** and **puku** which form large herds in the Luangwa Valley and Busanga Plains respectively. Both of these graceful antelope, with their chestnut coats and lyre-shaped horns, are similar in appearance to **lechwe** – a species adapted to life on seasonal flood plains. There are three varieties in Zambia (red, Kafue and black), each of them are largely confined to a particular wetland area.

WILDLIFE-WATCHING CALENDAR

Jan: height of the rains.
Feb: river safaris start in the Luangwa Valley.
Mar: storks and herons form large nesting colonies in South Luangwa National Park.
Apr: the Zambezi River reaches peak flood.
May: flood waters begin to recede from the plains around the Bangweulu Wetlands.
Jun: walking safari season begins in Luangwa Valley.
Jul: most camps have opened on the Busanga Plains in Kafue National Park.
Aug: storks, herons and other water birds feed on fish in shrinking pools.
Sep: carmine bee-eaters nest in South Luangwa National Park.
Oct: the wildebeest migration reaches Liuwa Plain National Park.
Nov: many varieties of birds are in breeding plumage.
Dec: mammals begin calving during the rainy season.

Below: *Although depleted by poachers in the 1970s and 1980s, elephants are still seen in Zambian national parks.*

Other antelope include the diminutive **duiker** and the stocky **eland**. Then there are **bushbuck**, **reedbuck**, **waterbuck**, **steenbok** and **grysbok** – and, of course, you should always keep an eye out for some of the more charismatic members of the family, like **blue wildebeest**, **Lichtenstein's hartebeest**, **sable**, **roan** and **kudu**.

Aardvark to Zebra

Don't worry if getting to grips with antelopes makes your head spin. Fortunately, Zambia's safari guides have a reputation for being some of the best in Africa. They will not only be able to identify any antelope on the hoof, but will know just the sort of places to look for other wildlife gems.

Admittedly, **aardvark** may be a challenge. You may well find the burrow of this strange, termite-eating creature, but it is strictly nocturnal and rarely seen.

As well as lion and leopard, **cats** in Zambia include **cheetah** and **serval** – beautiful, slender and spotted species best sought in Kafue National Park. The cat-like **civets** and **genets** also have distinctive markings. Despite being nocturnal, they are quite widespread and often glimpsed on night drives.

Dogs are represented in Zambia by the **side-striped jackal** and **African wild dog**, the latter being a rare but

Opposite: *The carmine bee-eater is a colourful summer visitor.*
Right: *Impala are widespread residents throughout Zambia.*

exhilarating sight in Kafue, Luiwa Plain or South Luangwa. The **spotted hyena** (dog-like, but more closely related to civets) is more common.

Zambia has its own unique sub-species of **giraffe** (Thornicroft's) which is restricted to the Luangwa Valley.

The **hippopotamus**, on the other hand, is found in rivers, lakes and swamps across the country. It is especially prolific in the Luangwa and Zambezi rivers.

The **mongoose** and **mustelid** families are also well represented. They include the widespread **banded mongoose** and the much rarer **honey badger** and **Cape clawless otter**.

Primates that you are almost guaranteed a sighting of are **baboon** and **vervet monkey**. The **blue monkey** is more restricted to forests in the north,

while the **bushbaby** is a curious nocturnal primate sometimes picked out on night drives by its large eyes that glow red in torchlight.

Rounding off the 'safari A–Z' are **warthog** and **zebra** – two favourites which are instantly identifiable and found throughout Zambia.

Bird Life

There are over 730 bird species recorded in Zambia. On safari, you will typically notice some of the larger or more colourful varieties, such as vultures, eagles, guineafowl, egrets and rollers. The key to bird-watching, however, is to visit a good range of habitats. Drive across open grassland and you may find cranes, bustards and the ground hornbill. Canoe along a river and you'll spot kingfishers, bee-eaters and the African fish eagle. Zambia also has rarities, like the shoebill stork of the Bangweulu Wetlands, while summer visitors include the beautiful carmine bee-eater.

Above: *Armed game scouts provide round-the-clock protection for white rhino in Mosi-oa-Tunya National Park.*

AFRICAN FISH EAGLE

Scientific name:
Haliaeetus vocifer
Vital statistics: wingspan up to 2.1m (7ft).
Distinguishing features: white head, chest, back and tail.
Habitat: lakes and rivers, often perching in pairs.
Diet: mainly fish which it snatches with outstretched talons.
Breeding: builds large stick nest used for many years.
Likes: throwing head back and calling with a ringing gull-like cry.
Dislikes: other fish eagles in its territory.

Conserving Zambia's Natural Heritage

During the 1970s and 1980s, Zambia's wildlife reeled from an onslaught of **poaching**. National parks provided little protection – even South Luangwa, the jewel in the crown, lost its black rhino. Elephant numbers crashed and wildlife everywhere became nervous and skittish.

Nowadays, poaching is largely under control and game populations in all the major parks have bounced back. Black rhino have been successfully reintroduced to North Luangwa National Park, while parts of the Bangweulu Wetlands are safeguarded by a joint project between the local community and the World Wide Fund for Nature.

Tourists can help to fuel the recovery of wildlife by staying at safari camps which have clear environmental aims, such as providing benefits to people living nearby. Involving **local communities** in nature conservation is crucial to the long-term future of Zambia's wildlife. It is unfair, unrealistic and unsustainable to advocate the preservation of animals purely for the benefit of a few privileged tourists if the local people remain excluded in poverty.

Wildlife must be seen to work harder for its place in today's Africa. There are now schemes in Zambia, for example, where a cut of the profits from upmarket safari operations is ploughed into new schools, health clinics and craft projects. If local people can see that wildlife improves their lives, they are more likely to help the conservationists' cause.

Near South Luangwa National Park, some villages have gone a step further by developing their own **cultural tourism** projects which can tap into the flow of safari-goers and directly boost their community incomes.

Big game hunting in Zambia's vast game management areas is another, albeit controversial, way of forging links between wildlife and people. Carefully controlled on a sustainable basis, it can generate local employment and income without adversely affecting animal populations.

National Parks

Zambia has 19 national parks administered by the Zambia Wildlife Authority (which replaced the National Parks and Wildlife Service in 1999). A few of the parks are extremely remote and have no visitor facilities. All of the following, however, have camps or lodges:

Lochinvar National Park is located 250km (155 miles) southwest of Lusaka and has an area of 428km² (165 sq miles) covering the flood plains of the Kafue Flats. Highlights include over 30,000 Kafue lechwe as well as abundant bird life.

Mosi-oa-Tunya National Park is located near Livingstone and has an area of 67km² (26 sq miles). Highlights include the eastern section of Victoria Falls, spectacular gorge scenery and a well-stocked game area.

Lower Zambezi National Park lies along the northern bank of the Zambezi east of Lusaka and has an area of 4092km² (1579 sq miles). Highlights include abundant elephant, buffalo and hippo, all of which can be observed on land or by canoe.

South Luangwa National Park is located in the Luangwa Valley east of Lusaka and has an area of 9050km² (3493 sq miles). It is one of Africa's finest reserves with abundant and varied wildlife that is best appreciated when going on a walking safari.

North Luangwa National Park has an area of 4636km² (1789 sq miles). Less visited than its southern

Below: *Open safari vehicles provide intimate encounters with Zambia's wildlife.*

Above: *This tree-top hide in Kasanka National Park is renowned for sightings of the rare sitatunga antelope.*
Opposite: *Kalambo Falls in northern Zambia is over twice the height of Victoria Falls.*

neighbour, it offers superb wilderness walking.

Kasanka National Park is located to the west of the Luangwa Valley and has an area of 390km² (150 sq miles). It has a special hide dubbed as Africa's best spot for watching the rare sitatunga antelope.

Sumbu National Park is located on the southwest shores of Lake Tanganyika and has an area of 2020km² (780 sq miles). It has varied game and excellent angling.

Nyika Plateau National Park is located in the northeast adjacent to the Malawian Nyika National Park and has an area of 80km² (31 sq miles). Highlights include hiking and horse riding across high plateau grassland.

Kafue National Park, Zambia's largest, is located west of Lusaka and has an area of 22,400km² (8646 sq miles). Highlights include Busanga Plains, diverse and abundant antelope and high predator numbers.

Liuwa Plain National Park is located in the far west and has an area of 3660km² (1413 sq miles). Its extensive grasslands are the setting for one of Africa's last undisturbed wildebeest migrations.

HISTORY IN BRIEF
Stone, Fire and Honey

Actual finds prove that humans lived in Zambia at least 250,000 years ago. Hand axes and other simple stone tools, sifted from deposits near **Victoria Falls**, suggest the existence of small nomadic groups that probably scavenged meat and collected berries and roots.

Intriguing evidence of early humans has also been unearthed at **Kabwe** where the 1921 discovery of a skull provided actual proof that people lived here around 125,000 years ago. This particular individual was proudly christened Broken Hill Man (after the old name for Kabwe), but discoveries to the east at **Kalambo Falls** were to prove

---

WHAT'S IN A NAME?

Baobab: variety of tree with enormous, bulbous trunk.
Dambo: shallow, grassy valley that is often waterlogged.
Kopje: granite outcrop on a plain.
Miombo: woodland dominated by Brachystegia trees.
Oxbow lake: semicircular lake formed when a meander is cut off from a river.
Pan: shallow, seasonal pool of water.
Riverine forest: strips of trees alongside rivers, also called gallery forest.

HISTORICAL CALENDAR

14th century Farming communities along the Zambezi River trade with Muslims from the East African coast.

17th–19th centuries Trading commodities include ivory, copper, gold and slaves.

1851 David Livingstone arrives in the Upper Zambezi.

1855 Livingstone renames *Mosi-oa-Tunya* ('Smoke that Thunders') as the Victoria Falls.

1873 Livingstone dies in the Bangweulu Wetlands.

1891 Imperialist and millionaire Cecil Rhodes proclaims the territories of Southern Rhodesia (Zimbabwe) and Northern Rhodesia (Zambia).

1902 European prospector,

William Collier, 'discovers' Northern Rhodesia's vast copper deposits.

1924 British Colonial Office takes political control of Northern Rhodesia.

1930s Large-scale commercial exploitation of Northern Rhodesia's copper begins.

1952 Northern Rhodesia African Mineworkers' Union go on strike for better pay.

1953 Northern Rhodesia, Southern Rhodesia and Nyasaland become part of Central African Federation.

1958 Kenneth Kaunda's Zambia African National Congress is banned.

1960 Kaunda takes leadership

of the United National Independence Party.

1963 The Central African Federation collapses.

1964 Zambia is declared independent with Kenneth Kaunda as president.

1991 Frederick Chiluba of the Movement for Multiparty Democracy becomes president.

2001 Levy Mwanawasa is elected as president.

2003 Former President Chiluba is arrested and charged with corruption.

2005 World Bank approves $3.8 billion of debt relief for Zambia.

2006 Mwanawasa wins second term in government.

equally exciting. Scientists here have found evidence of prehistoric fire. Its association with early Stone-Age artefacts sparks a tantalizing hypothesis that humans had discovered how to make fire in this corner of Africa at least 60,000 years ago.

Armed with such a useful skill, not to mention an ever more sophisticated array of tools and weapons (including the bow and arrow), late Stone-Age people became adept hunter-gatherers. They may well have resembled the present-day San whose traditional lifestyles now exist only in the central Kalahari. Certainly they shared the San's penchant for rock paintings – schematic designs have been found in **Nsalu Cave** that are 12,000 years old. And, judging by the tooth decay found in some skeletons, they were equally fond of honey!

Opposite: *A mural in Livingstone's National Museum captures life in an early rural community.*
Below: *The Scottish missionary-explorer, Dr David Livingstone, strikes an epic pose in a statue at Victoria Falls.*

The First Farmers

Whether late Stone-Age rock art in Zambia was spiritual or merely decorative remains a mystery. Whatever its purpose, by around 300BC, it started to fade – along with its makers.

Migrating from the north, Iron-Age farmers proved overwhelmingly efficient in the Stone-Age culture of Zambia. These ancestors of modern black Africans had mastered something even greater than fire – they had learned how to cultivate crops and domesticate animals. Furthermore, they were miners and metal-workers. Iron axes were used to clear forests for agriculture, while Zambia's copper began to be excavated – not so much for tools, but as a trading commodity.

Iron-Age communities in Zambia were trading at least as early as AD1400. At **Ing'ombe Ilede**, a short distance downstream from the present-day **Kariba Dam**, excavations revealed an Iron-Age settlement littered with copper crosses, gold ingots, and glass beads. It was clear that, as the first Zambian chiefdoms became established, they were trading goods with the outside world.

Traders and Slavers

Muslim traders from the East African coast were probably the first to venture as far as Zambia. However, by the 17th century the Portuguese were making inroads from Mozambique. At first, gold, copper, rhino horn and ivory fuelled the trade – but slaves were soon to be added to the list of commodities. Intertribal conflict ensured a ready supply and, by the early 19th century, slaves were in huge demand by emerging industrial powers in Europe and North America.

On God's Highway

A Scotsman called **David Livingstone** was appalled by what he saw of the slave trade in the early 1850s when he first travelled to the Upper Zambezi. The young missionary believed that only a combination of Christianity and self-sufficient commerce would eradicate the grizzly business. His idea was to export locally abundant and legitimate products, like cotton, to overseas markets. Livingstone felt this trade could be most easily channelled through the Portuguese port of Luanda in present-day Angola. But when he tested the route it proved totally unsuitable.

Livingstone then turned his attention eastwards. Perhaps the Zambezi River could be 'God's Highway' to the Indian Ocean instead. With renewed enthusiasm, the missionary-explorer set off on his second great expedition. In 1855 he renamed **Mosi-oa-Tunya** ('The Smoke that Thunders') as **Victoria Falls**. Everything seemed to be going to plan when Livingstone finally reached the coast. Returning to England, he published *Missionary Travels and Researches in South Africa* (an instant best-seller), and was appointed leader of a new expedition to make God's Highway a reality. However, once again, the route proved impossible. Livingstone had overlooked the **Kebrabasa Rapids**. God's Highway was impassable.

A decade later, in the mid-1860s, Livingstone was back in Africa searching for the source of the Nile. It was to prove a final futile and tragic quest. Lost in the **Bangweulu Wetlands** and suffering from dysentery, Livingstone died near **Chitambo Village** in 1873 (*see page 94*).

The Scramble for Africa

Livingstone's epic journeys were by no means in vain. His travels opened the way for other missionaries and ex-plorers, but events to the south and west were about to trigger an all-out scramble for control of southern Africa.

Britain had already claimed the Cape, while Boers were scattered across the Transvaal. However, when Germany annexed South West Africa (now Namibia) in 1884, the British grew uneasy about a potential German-Boer alliance. In response, they ratified the British Protectorate

DR LIVINGSTONE

Born on 19 March 1813 at Blantyre, Scotland, David Livingstone was 10 when he began work at a cotton mill on the River Clyde. By 1840, how-ever, he had a medical degree and was sailing to Africa as a missionary. At Kuruman Mission, he met future wife, Mary, and began the first of several epic journeys during which he recorded the Zambezi River, Victoria Falls, Lake Ngami and Lake Malawi. In 1865, Livingstone set out on a fruitless search for the source of the Nile. New York journalist Henry Stanley found the explorer in 1871, greeting him with the immortal words 'Dr Livingstone, I presume?' Livingstone succumbed to dysentery in the Bangweulu swamps on 1 May 1873. His heart was buried nearby, while followers Sussi and Chuma carried his body to the coast. Livingstone was interred at Westminster Abbey and his National Memorial stands on the banks of the River Clyde.

Above: *Workers at an opencast mine in Zambia's Copperbelt region.*

of Bechuanaland (now Botswana) and later authorized the millionaire imperialist, Cecil Rhodes, to seek land treaties with chiefs to the north and east.

By now, gold had been discovered in the Witwatersrand and diamonds at Kimberley. Rhodes already had control of the latter and was dreaming of a far bigger prize – to link the Cape with Cairo under British rule. In return for 'colonial protection', the chiefs capitulated to Rhodes' demands for exclusive mining rights on their land. By 1891, Rhodes' British South Africa Company had proclaimed the territories of Southern Rhodesia (Zimbabwe) and Northern Rhodesia (Zambia).

At first, Northern Rhodesia yielded little in the way of mineral wealth. Instead it was exploited for labour to work the lucrative gold and diamond mines further south. New taxes forced people into the cash economy and, by the early 1900s, a railway link from Northern Rhodesia to Kimberley was transporting thousands of involuntary workers. By 1911, **Livingstone** was established as Northern Rhodesia's capital (*see* page 45).

Red Gold

In 1923, Southern Rhodesia became self-governing and, a year later, the British Colonial Office took political control of Northern Rhodesia from the British South Africa Company. Africans remained very much on the sidelines of these developments. Even when the rich deposits of the **Copperbelt** began to be heavily exploited in the 1930s (*see* page 36), Africans were subjected to appalling working conditions, poor wages and little training or education. Deaths in the mines were common and this, coupled with the relentless recruitment of workers, caused depopulation, poverty and malnutrition in rural areas.

SIR CECIL JOHN RHODES (1853–1902)

1871 Arrives in South Africa to work for his brother.
1888 Founds De Beers Consolidated Mines (mining 90 per cent of world's diamonds by 1891).
1889 Takes charge of British South Africa Company.
1890 Becomes Premier of Cape Colony.
1891 Proclaims Northern and Southern Rhodesia.
1895 Plots to overthrow Transvaal President, SJP Kruger – but fails.
1896 Resigns as Premier of Cape Colony.

It wasn't long before the first rumbles of dissent began to be heard. African miners staged a strike in 1935 – the same year that **Lusaka** became the capital. However, it was not until 1952 that a fledgling Northern Rhodesia African Mineworkers' Union actually succeeded in negotiating better pay and conditions for its members.

Meanwhile, other sweeping political changes were afoot. Resenting revenue-draining colonial rule and feeling threatened by the increasing power wielded by miners, white settlers in Northern and Southern Rhodesia formed the independent Central African Federation with Nyasaland (now Malawi) in 1953.

GEMSTONES

Zambia is one of the world's leading producers of emeralds and other precious stones. Retail outlets selling amethyst, aquamarine, emerald, tourmaline, garnet and ruby can be found in Lusaka's Inter-Continental and Holiday Inn hotels. Be wary of unscrupulous dealers. Street sellers have been known to offer green traffic-light glass as emeralds!

Towards Independence

Not surprisingly, the Federation was bitterly opposed by the black population. Forged from various welfare groups, a new political movement called the Northern Rhodesia African National Congress had fought its imposition every step of the way. Despite its failure to stop the Federation, African resistance spawned ever more dynamic activists. Among them was Kenneth Kaunda – a schoolteacher who would eventually lead Northern Rhodesia to independence.

In 1958, Kaunda's first efforts were severely quashed. His Zambia African National Congress was banned and its leaders imprisoned. Two years later, however, Kaunda was free and in control of another party called the United National Independence Party (UNIP). Backed by the now powerful mining trade unions, UNIP's drive towards independence became unstoppable. In 1963, the Federation collapsed. The following year, Northern Rhodesia held its first elections based on universal adult suffrage. Inevitably, UNIP swept to power and on 24 October 1964, Kenneth Kaunda became president of independent Zambia.

Below: *Gemstones mined in Zambia include emerald, amethyst, aquamarine, tourmaline, garnet and rose quartz.*

The Kaunda Government

Following the elation of gaining independence, Kaunda's government was brought crashing to earth by a few harsh realities. Independent Zambia had problems. Not only was it saddled with massive debt, but its population was largely uneducated and most of its trade had to pass south through Rhodesia (Zimbabwe) – now under white independent rule and struggling to endure overseas sanctions.

Desperate to open up new trade routes, Kaunda endorsed plans for road and rail links with Tanzania. Revenue from copper was ploughed into new schools, employment and food subsidies. But in the early 1970s, world copper prices plummeted, crippling the country's already floundering economy. Zambia's finances buckled under international debt and the country sank into the league of the world's poorest nations.

Notwithstanding the copper crisis and Kaunda's efforts to improve the country's infrastructure, Zambia's misfortunes were not helped by the government's reputation for autocracy, inefficiency and corruption. Opposition was inevitable and Kaunda's 27-year rule was ended in November 1991 when Frederick Chiluba's Movement for Multiparty Democracy (MMD) swept to power with 84 per cent of the vote.

The Chiluba Government

Below: *The flag of the Republic of Zambia.*

Inheriting a foreign debt of nearly US$7 billion, Chiluba set a radical reform of the economy, implementing a free market and new investment laws, as well as a stock exchange and a programme of privatization.

But debt still weighed heavily on Zambia. Chiluba's long-term plans for the country's recovery, although positive and welcome, were shrouded with suspicion during his 1996 election victory when constitutional tinkering was suspected. This, together with a heavy-handed response to a half-hearted coup in 1997, cooled relations with international donors and human rights groups.

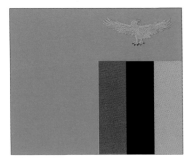

The Mwanawasa Government

Frederick Chiluba was succeeded as president by the MMD's Levy Mwanawasa during the 2001 elections. Mwanawasa was elected with less than 30 per cent of the vote, and independent EU monitors raised concerns over flaws in counting procedures and administration. Zambia's new president was immediately faced with tackling issues like rife unemployment and inflation, not to mention the alarming spread of HIV/AIDS.

On a more positive note, Mwanawasa inherited a new Zambia Wildlife Authority and steadily growing tourism numbers. In 2005, the World Bank approved a US$3.8 billion debt relief package to write off more than 50% of Zambia's debt.

In 2006, Mwanawasa suffered a minor stroke, but later declared himself fit for re-election towards the end of the year. Following a high turn-out at the polls in September, he won a second term in government.

GOVERNMENT AND ECONOMY

Anyone over 18 years of age is eligible to vote in Zambia. The country's National Assembly is composed of 150 elected representatives from which the president (who is both chief of state and head of government) appoints cabinet ministers.

Zambia has nine administrative divisions or provinces – Central, Copperbelt, Eastern, Luapula, Lusaka, Northern, Northwestern, Southern and Western. The legal system is based on English common law and customary law.

Infrastructure

Beyond urban centres and major routes, Zambia's road network is poor and quickly becomes impassable during the height of summer rains. There are, however, more than one hundred airports and airfields scattered across the country, enabling quick and relatively simple access to even the most remote regions. Something of a feat for a landlocked country, Zambia has one port, Mpulungu, serving the ferry routes on Lake Tanganyika. Rail islimited to the Tanzania–Zambia Railway (TAZARA) and a domestic

NATIONAL ANTHEM

Stand and sing of Zambia
  proud and free,
Land of works and joy in unity,
Victors in the struggle for
  the right,
We have won freedom's fight.
All one, strong and free.

Africa is our own motherland,
Fashioned with and blessed
  by God's good hand.
Let us all her people join
  as one,
Brothers under the sun,
All one, strong and free.

One land and one nation
  is our cry,
Dignity and peace 'neath
  the Zambian sky.
Like our noble eagle in
  its flight,
Zambia, praise to thee,
All one, strong and free.

Praise to God, Bless our
  great nation,
Free men we stand,
Under the flag of our land,
Zambia, praise to thee,
All one, strong and free.

line connecting Lusaka with Livingstone and the Copperbelt.

Industry

Zambia's main industry is **mining**. It is the world's largest producer of cobalt and the fourth largest producer of copper. Coal and high-quality emeralds are also mined commercially.

Domestic **energy** is provided by several hydro-electric power stations, including those at Kariba Dam and Victoria Falls. Surplus power is exported. **Agriculture** is one of the country's biggest employers and generates exports of tobacco, vegetables, fruit, coffee, tea and ornamental flowers. Other domestic farming products include maize, sorghum, rice, peanuts, sunflower seeds, cotton, sugar cane, cassava, cattle, goats, pigs, poultry and eggs. **Manufacturing industries** mainly produce textiles and cement. **Tourism**, largely backed by private investment, is concentrated in the Victoria Falls region and major national parks.

THE PEOPLE

Zambia has a population of around 11.5 million which roughly equates to 15 people per square kilometre – one of the lowest land to population ratios in Africa. This sparseness of density is further exacerbated by the fact that urban centres are home to nearly half the population, leaving thinly inhabited rural areas and large tracts of empty wilderness.

Religion

The vast majority of the population are black Africans, with just over one per cent of European or Indian origin. Around 60 per cent are Christians, with the remainder being Muslims or Hindus. Indigenous beliefs are also followed, either exclusively or as part of another religion.

TRADITIONAL CEREMONIES

February: Lwiinde is celebrated by the Leya people of the Livingstone region who make sacrifices for rain to their ancestral spirits in Batoka Gorge. N'cwala is a thanksgiving festival held on the 24th near Chipata.

February/March : Ku-omboka celebrates the seasonal migration of the Lozi people from the Barotse Flood Plains to higher ground, with the king leading a spectacular flotilla on his royal barge.

July: Umotomboka, held in Luapula Province, commemorates the arrival of Chief Mwata Kazembe's people from the Congo and is accompanied by the chief's sword dance and much feasting.

August: Likumbe Liyamize celebrates the cultural heritage of the Luvale people in northwest Zambia. Lukuni Luzwa Buuka is an ancient Toka ceremony depicting their conquest of other tribes.

September: Shimunenga is a god to whom the Ba-Ila people offer thanks over the period of the full moon.

Language

Although Zambia's official language is English, over 70 dialects of Bantu origin have been identified in at least 16 cultural groups across the country. **Bemba**, the largest of these, is concentrated around Lusaka and the Copperbelt where it is used in education and administration. **Nyanja** is also widespread, but it is more of a universal kind of lingua franca than a traditional language. **Tonga** is much older and widely used in the Zambezi Valley, while **Lozi** is confined mainly to the west around Barotseland. Other major dialects include **Kaonde** (in the central northeast), **Lunda** (in the Copperbelt), **Luvale** (in the far northwest), **Nsenga** (in the southeast) and **Tumbuka** (in the far east).

> ### WEDDINGS
>
> *Lobola* (the bride price) is still widely practised in Zambia. Weddings are long and lively affairs, with much food, drink, dancing and drumming taking place over two or three days.

Traditional Culture

Although Zambia has an ethnically diverse background, many of the country's individual cultures have been blurred by western influences, intermarriage between tribal groups and a trend towards urban migration. That's not to say, however, that Zambia is bereft of indigenous culture. Far from it. In fact, following independence, various schemes were launched to preserve local heritage through **cultural villages and museums**. Interesting displays of traditional artefacts and crafts can be seen at Choma Museum, Maramba Cultural Centre in Livingstone, Moto Moto Museum in Mbala, and Nayuma Museum in Mongu.

In some rural areas, cultural practices have remained largely unchanged for centuries – a prime example being **Barotseland** in Zambia's far west. Here, the Lozi people maintain a tradition of annual migration to escape the seasonal floods of the Upper Zambezi. The departure of the Lozi king and his entourage is part of the **Ku-omboka**, Zambia's most spectacular traditional ceremony which

Opposite: *The Bemba, comprising around 18 per cent of Zambia's population, have a paramount chief called the Chitimukulu.*
Below: *This church in Zambia's Luapula Province was built in the early 1900s by the London Missionary Society.*

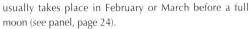

GREETINGS

When talking to a Zambian begin any conversation, no matter how brief or urgent, with a greeting, followed by a polite enquiry, such as 'How are you?' If you can manage this in a native tongue, so much the better! Greetings are usually followed by a handshake (often a slick, three-stage movement which you will quickly learn). A man should withhold his hand until the woman offers hers.

usually takes place in February or March before a full moon (see panel, page 24).

Most of Zambia's traditional ceremonies take place in fairly remote locations, and their actual dates can be hard to pin down. This probably explains why few visitors get to witness them – it's a case of being in the right place at the right time. However, the **Livingstone Cultural & Arts Festival**, first held in 1994, is destined to become a focus for cultural activity in Zambia. Attracting musicians, artists, poets and dramatists from across the country, it provides both visitors and locals with an insight into Zambia's cultural diversity.

Perhaps the most enlightening way to experience everyday rural culture is to spend some time in a typical village. Tour operators in the Victoria Falls area can arrange visits to nearby villages, but one project in the

Luangwa Valley has become internationally renowned for offering visitors the chance to actually take part in traditional life. **Kawaza Village** (see page 85) is home to the Kunda tribe who migrated from the Luba area in Congo during the early 1800s. Traditionally they were hunters, but most now live as subsistence farmers – a lifestyle constantly at odds with extreme seasons and crop-raiding wildlife.

In 1997, Kawaza Village had introduced cultural tourism, not as a profit-making scheme, but as an opportunity to exchange ideas and cultures with foreigners and to raise money for community development projects. Guests not only sleep in traditional huts and eat local food, but also take part in daily activities, such as collecting water, grinding the maize, brewing the beer or consulting a traditional healer.

A large part of Zambian culture is fused with **music and dance**. Traditional dancing is often accompanied by vibrant, rhythmic drumming and whistling. As well as drums, popular instruments include the thumb piano and *silimba* – like a xylophone with wooden keys mounted over gourds. Dance, of course, is equally entrenched in urban lives. Many nightclubs and shebeens pulse to the beat of the rumba.

Arts and Crafts

For many visitors, the most obvious expression of Zambian culture lies in the stunning variety of arts and crafts found throughout the country. Craft and curio stalls can be found in all the main tourist centres, particularly Livingstone. Wooden carvings of animals seem particularly abundant – probably as a result of tourist demand rather than tradition.

Basketry, however, has deep cultural roots. Practised by both men and women, there are many different styles reflecting both the environment in which they are made and the intended use. Raw materials include grass, bark, bamboo, sisal, palm leaves and liana vines. Many baskets are decorated with symbolic designs using dyes made from soil, bark, roots and leaves. They are used for anything from sieving maize flour and trapping fish to storage and tableware.

Carving is usually only undertaken by men. Some superbly crafted animals, masks, drums, bowls, furniture and walking sticks are produced. Wood is not the only raw material used. Soapstone and malachite are fashioned into a bewildering array of chess sets, hippos and modern sculptures. For something perhaps a little more meaningful, look out for Nyaminyami sticks – wooden carvings depicting the serpent-headed guardian of the Zambezi River.

Pottery is less commonly encountered on the typical curio stalls, but it forms an intrinsic part of local culture, with the first evidence of its use in Zambia dating back to the Iron Age. In Lusaka, the Moore Pottery produces some beautiful pots and ceramics. Raw materials are all sourced locally and include clay from the Mkushi River and feldspar from

Above: *Zambian carving and basketry is among the finest in Africa.*
Opposite: *As well as in tourist displays, dancing and drumming play important roles in rituals, ceremonies and celebrations.*

BEST BUYS

There is a bewildering range of souvenirs for sale in Zambia and around Victoria Falls, from T-shirts proclaiming 'I survived the Zambezi's rapids' to simple but exquisite baskets made in remote rural villages. Try to support various community projects which encourage local villagers to develop art and craft projects. Tribal Textiles in South Luangwa, for example, produce beautiful wall hangings, as well as wire animal sculptures made from confiscated snares.

Above: *Polo is a popular sport in Zambia, particularly among the small expatriate community.*

Kapiri Moshi. The glazes also evoke a strong affinity with Zambia, with naturally occurring minerals being used to create rich ochres and reds.

Contemporary and traditional art is also extremely well represented in the capital's many galleries. Those with a particular interest in African art, however, should make a point of visiting Chaminuka Lodge located on a private nature reserve north of Lusaka. Here, an outstanding private collection gathered over 50 years provides a superb cross section of paintings, sculptures, artefacts and antiques from more than 35 African countries. Renowned Zambian artists are well represented, with work by Flinto Chandia, Petson Lombe, Peter Maibwe, Patrick Mumba, Godfrey Setti, Shadreck Simukanga and Henry Tiyali.

Sport and Recreation

Zambians are passionate about **soccer**. In even the most remote villages children can be seen kicking around rudimentary footballs made from tied bundles of rags. Most towns and villages have their own teams, while the national side is fervently supported. Zambia's soccer heroes include Kalusha Bwalya, a former African Footballer of the Year. Tragically, several talented players were killed on 17 April 1993 when the plane carrying the Zambian World Cup team crashed in the sea off Gabon.

Boxing is another popular sport in Zambia. Lottie Mwale is a former Commonwealth light-heavyweight boxing champion, while Keith Mwila won an Olympic bronze medal in the flyweight category.

Other competitive sports include **rugby**, **golf** and **polo**. Lilayi Lodge, near Lusaka, offers polo holidays, while the city's showgrounds host matches at the weekends.

One of the most popular pastimes in Zambia is **angling**. Lake Kariba is within easy reach of Lusaka and makes an excellent weekend fishing break. Other sections of the Zambezi River are also renowned angling

PERFECT NSIMA

To make *nsima*, the staple food for Zambians, you will need four cups of water and two cups of plain corn meal (for four servings). Pour the water into a cooking pot or saucepan and heat until lukewarm. One tablespoon at a time, slowly add three-quarters of the corn meal, stirring continuously until the mixture begins to boil and thicken. Turn heat to medium, cover and simmer for around three minutes. Gradually add the remainder of the corn meal and stir until smooth. Cover, remove from heat and allow to stand for another three minutes. Serve hot with a vegetable, bean, meat or fish dish.

spots, particularly the Barotse Flood Plains on the Upper Zambezi and the Batoka Gorge and stretches of the Lower Zambezi downstream of Victoria Falls. Lake Tanganyika also offers superb fishing.

Although **chess** was given a boost in Zambia when the country's 16-year-old Amon Simutowe won the South African Open Chess Championship, the traditional board game of **isolo** remains a firm favourite. It is played on a wooden board partitioned into several chambers containing stones which opponents try to capture.

In rural areas, children combine limited resources with wonderful imagination to create a variety of games. Boys fashion scraps of wire into detailed 'push-along' toy cars, complete with bottle tops for wheels, while girls play nchuba – a catching game requiring fast reflexes.

Food and Drink

Zambia offers a wide range of cuisine. The staple dish is called nsima, a steamed cornmeal mash made from ground maize. Visitors should try some – it is particularly tasty when accompanied by a meat or vegetable sauce. A more acquired taste is the opaque and frothy village-brewed beer, known as chibuku or 'shake-shake.'

In safari camps and lodges, dishes are typically international with a local twist. They might include fresh fish in a European-style sauce followed by a sponge dessert using local fruit. Standards always seem to be extremely high – no matter how remote the camp. In large towns and cities you will find everything from takeaways and street stalls to Chinese restaurants and salad bars.

In addition to the standard range of soft drinks, Zambia offers two main bottled beers (Mosi and Rhino), as well as various good quality southern African wines.

LOCAL FOOD

Zambia's staple food is a thick cornmeal mash called nsima. It is made by pounding maize kernels using a large mortar and pestle, and then adding water. Nsima may be served for breakfast with milk and sugar or for dinner with fish, meat or beans – often with a tomato and onion relish and a side serving of pumpkin or cassava. Nsima na nkuku is a popular chicken dish.

Most villages brew their own beer which is usually thick, frothy and potent. Umunkoyo is a non-alcoholic drink made from roots.

Below: *Traditional Zambian food consists of cornmeal mash accompanied by fish, meat, beans or a tomato and onion relish.*

2
Lusaka and Central Zambia

For many visitors to Zambia, Lusaka is viewed simply as an arrival and departure point – somewhere to transit as quickly as possible to and from the country's spectacular natural wonders. It is true that, like many capital cities, Lusaka is chaotic, overcrowded and somewhat bewildering. But no-one can doubt the relentless energy of the place. If you are looking for 'the real Africa' it is just as likely to be found in a bustling Lusaka marketplace as it is in a remote national park.

Those who dismiss Zambia's capital too swiftly will miss several interesting **museums** and cultural highlights, including a range of local **art and craft galleries**. Lusaka does not, perhaps, lend itself to the traditional 'city tour', but it does nonetheless deserve a day or two of browsing.

A short distance from the city are several **nature reserves** and **farm lodges** which can provide a relaxing and interesting 'taster' of the kind of the wildlife you can expect to find on a forthcoming safari.

Venturing further afield, the Great North Road links Lusaka with the industrial mining towns of the **Copperbelt**. Again, perhaps not immediately inspiring, but there are several interesting nuggets to be teased from a trip north, including **mine visits**, **Chembe Bird Sanctuary** and the **Chimfunshi Wildlife Orphanage**.

South of Lusaka, the road to Livingstone passes close to **Lochinvar National Park**, a natural gem which protects part of the Kafue River's flood plain. Here, you will find incredible bird life, plus many Kafue lechwe – antelope specially adapted to life on the waterlogged plains.

DON'T MISS

** **Lusaka:** browse the art and craft galleries, visit a local market or treat yourself to a stay at a nearby luxury private nature reserve.
** **Chimfunshi Wildlife Orphanage:** a remarkable rehabilitation centre for orphaned chimpanzees.
** **Lochinvar National Park:** a bird-watcher's paradise on the flood plains of the Kafue River.

Opposite: *Zambia's modern capital city is a stark contrast to its wilderness national parks.*

LUSAKA

Like all large cities, arriving in Lusaka can be confusing. Try to orientate yourself using two of the capital's main roads – Cairo Road (a busy shopping area near the railway station and bus terminal) and Independence Avenue which runs east towards a less frenetic district scattered with embassies and international hotels. City street maps can be purchased from Mulungushi House, just off Independence Avenue, opposite the US Embassy. Useful information, including where to eat and what's on, can be found in a monthly magazine called *Lusaka Lowdown*, now also available at www.lowdown.co.zm

Security

Although Lusaka's reputation for crime is probably exaggerated, you should still take the same precautions as you would in any city. Walking around at night is asking for unwanted attention. During the day, avoid flaunting large sums of cash or expensive camera equipment – particularly when visiting local markets when valuables are best left in your hotel safe.

Below: *Buses from Lusaka ply routes to Livingstone, Ndola and other main towns in Zambia.*

National Museum ★★

Located on Independence Avenue, the National Museum provides an interesting insight into Zambia's cultural history. There are displays of various artefacts and contemporary art and sculpture, as well as an intriguing section on witchcraft. Museum is open daily, 09:00–16:30, closed on public holidays.

Political Museum ★

Zambia's struggle for independence is portrayed in this museum situated in Mulungushi Hall, Great East Road. Museum is open daily, 09:00–16:30.

Kabwata Cultural Centre ★

This collection of ronda-vels near Burma Road is a focus for traditional carving (in both wood and stone) and occasional dancing. A range of curios is available at good prices. Open daily, 07:00–18:00.

Zintu Community Museum ★★

Indigenous arts and crafts are displayed in this museum on Panganini Road, providing a fascinating cross section of Zambia's creative heritage. Open Mon–Fri, 09:00–16:30, Sat, 09:00–13:00.

Kalimba Reptile Park ★

A short drive from the city along the Great East Road, turning left before the airport, Kalimba Reptile Park houses a variety of African snakes, crocodiles, tortoises and chameleons. Open daily, 09:00–17:30.

Mundawanga Environmental Park ★★

Formerly a rather run-down zoo and botanical garden, Mundawanga Environmental Park (located out of town on the Kafue Road) is being transformed into a more modern wildlife centre with the emphasis on indigenous species and education. Old cages and concrete pens are making way for new 'zones' depicting Zambia's various habitats. Open daily, 08:00–17:00.

Other Attractions

The following may be of interest if you are passing: the National Archives (Government Road), the Cathedral of the Holy Cross and Freedom Statue (Independence Avenue) and Parliament Buildings (Nangwenya Road).

Above: *Be prepared to haggle hard, but fairly, in Lusaka's craft markets.*
Opposite: *Lechwe Lodge and other private reserves near Lusaka provide an oasis of calmness after the hectic pace of the capital.*

Art Galleries ★★

Lusaka has a liberal scattering of galleries and studios which reflect the city's numerous and talented artists. Located 15km (9 miles) from the city centre along the Leopard's Hill Road, **Namwandwe Gallery** contains an excellent collection of paintings, sculptures, ceramics and textiles representing Zambia's foremost artists, including Henry Tayali. It is open on Tue–Sun. Other fine displays can be found at the **Bente Lorentz Ceramic Studio** in Longacres, the **Henry Tayali Visual Arts Centre** at the Showgrounds, **Mpala Gallery** on Mwilwa Road, and the **Moore Pottery** on Kabelenga Road. Visitors to **Chaminuka Nature Reserve** can view a spectacular collection of paintings and artefacts from more than 35 African countries.

Local Markets ★★

As much a visual and cultural experience as an opportunity to go shopping, Lusaka's local markets are crowded, lively and fascinating. Just remember to be especially wary of theft. The city's three main markets are Kamwala, Central and New City.

Shopping ★

If you are looking for curios, such as baskets and carvings, Kabwata Cultural Village may well provide the best bargains. Several of the galleries and museums also have sales outlets. Also worth perusing are the gemstones and jewellery displayed in shops at major hotels, such as the Holiday Inn and Inter-Continental.

CLIMATE

Located on the northern side of the Kafue River, **Blue Lagoon National Park** lies roughly opposite Lochinvar National Park and contains similar flood plains, herds of lechwe and large numbers of birds. To visit this wetland reserve, however, you will need to be totally self-sufficient as there are no tourist facilities.

Nature Reserves and Farm Lodges ★★★

A short drive from Lusaka, several private nature reserves and farm lodges offer a peaceful retreat from the city. If you are on a very tight itinerary, they also provide the chance to view some of Zambia's wonderful wildlife without visiting the larger, more remote national parks.

Located 45km (28 miles) north of Lusaka, **Chaminuka Nature Reserve** supports a remarkable variety of animals in a reserve just 35km² (14 sq miles) in area. As well as antelope, such as eland, sable and roan, there are lion, cheetah and hyena housed in separate enclosures. Activities include game drives, bush walks, horse riding, fishing and boating. The lodge also contains an extensive African art collection.

Also north of the capital, **Protea Hotel Lusaka Safari Lodge** is set in a private reserve of 12km² (5 sq miles) which includes a lake where you can watch various antelope come to drink. The reserve also has four lions (in an enclosure) and an orphaned elephant called Mphanvu.

South of the capital, on a similarly sized farm on the banks of the Kafue River, **Lechwe Lodge** provides an excellent chance of spotting antelope, zebra and giraffe. As well as game-viewing, the lodge can arrange boating, horse riding and fishing.

About 20km (12 miles) south of Lusaka, **Lilayi Lodge** is situated on a game ranch stocked with antelope, giraffe and zebra. Night drives organized by the lodge sometimes reveal more unusual species, such as porcupine or aardvark. Other activities include walks, bird-watching, horse riding and excursions to view the Zambezi Valley from the top of the escarpment.

COPPER PROPERTIES

Copper has many remarkable properties. It can be rolled into sheets just 0.13mm (0.005in) thick and drawn into wire thinner than human hair. Copper is also an excellent conductor of both electricity and heat. It is resistant to rust and reaches melting point at 1083°C (1981°F).

Below: *Despite collapsing copper prices, the Copperbelt is Zambia's industrial heartland.*

NORTH TOWARDS THE COPPERBELT

Road and rail lead north from Zambia's capital into the country's industrial heartland. While not a typical tourist route, the copper and cobalt mining towns of Ndola, Kitwe and Chingola have enough of interest to make a trip worthwhile – particularly if combined with further forays to one or two excellent wildlife spots.

History

In 1902, a European prospector called William Collier 'discovered' Zambia's vast copper deposits while out hunting roan antelope. A memorial named in his honour can be seen at the Roan Antelope Mine in Luanshya. Notwithstanding Collier's achievement, it is worth pointing out that copper had, in fact, been exploited in the region since at least the 7th century. There is even evidence that early Iron-Age people excavated the mineral, fashioned it into bangles and traded it with their neighbours.

It was not until after World War I, however, that small-scale commercial copper mining began. Demand grew rapidly, transforming the economy of what was then Northern Rhodesia. With larger, more efficient mines pockmarking the Copperbelt, 'red gold' soon dominated the country's exports. Even today, with collapsing copper prices, the industry still accounts for over half of Zambia's export earnings and more than a tenth of its labour force.

Highlights

The first main town on the road north from Lusaka is **Kabwe**. Originally known as Broken Hill, its main claim to fame is the extraordinary discovery, during mining excavations in 1921, of a prehistoric human skull (*see* page 16). Christened 'Broken Hill

Man', the specimen was dated at around 125,000 years old – the earliest human remains ever found in southern Africa.

Further to the northwest, **Ndola** is a large industrial and commercial centre. The **Copperbelt Museum** in Buteko Avenue contains a selection of minerals found in the surrounding area. You can also purchase copper curios here. On Makoli Avenue the **Slave Tree** (a mishmash of mahogany and parasitic fig) was once used as a meeting place for 19th-century slave traders.

On the road between Ndola and **Kitwe** the **Dag Hammarskjöld Memorial** commemorates the point where the former United Nations Secretary General died in a plane crash in 1961. Kitwe itself has few landmarks – although it is possible to take a **mine tour**.

Approximately 30km (19 miles) south of Kitwe, near the town of Kalalushi, **Chembe Bird Sanctuary** is a different kind of treasure in this mining region. Run by the Wildlife and Environmental Conservation Society of Zambia (*see* page 13), the sanctuary's woodland and lake supports a wealth of birds.

Back on the main road heading west, **Chingola** signals the end of the Copperbelt with one of Africa's largest **opencast mines**. With a permit from the mine office in Fern Avenue you can visit the mine. Or you might prefer a walk in the more salubrious surroundings of the **Nchanga Golf Course**.

Chimfunshi Wildlife Orphanage ★★

Threatened by poachers and deforestation throughout their range, chimpanzees find sanctuary at this remarkable orphanage 67km (42 miles) west of Chingola. Established by David and Sheila Siddle in 1983, Chimfunshi rescues

Above: *Boats can be hired for fishing or bird-watching at Chembe Bird Sanctuary.*

SAFARI POTPOURRI

On safari, in addition to well-known species like elephant, zebra, lion, buffalo, warthog, baboon, crocodile and hippo, you'll see a range of antelopes and smaller animals, such as mongooses and tree squirrels. With luck, you may also see leopard, cheetah and giraffe. To maximize your chances of spotting a range of species, you should explore a variety of habitats – river, woodland, grassland, etc -- and, if possible, include a night drive. Nocturnal creatures include bushbaby, jackal and genet. Bird-watching is also wonderful on safari. With binoculars and a guidebook, you'll spot everything from gawky vultures to iridescent bee-eaters.

Above: *Chimfunshi Wildlife Orphanage runs a highly successful re-habilitation programme for chimpanzees.*

orphaned wild chimps, as well as those condemned to misery in dilapidated zoos around the world.

As part of a highly successful rehabilitation programme (which has resulted in numerous births at the centre), new arrivals are gradually introduced to one of five social groups. These are allowed to roam freely across large enclosures containing thick forest and open grassland.

In addition to over 100 chimpanzees, Chimfunshi has nursed back to health everything from birds to hippos. An environmental education centre for local children was opened in 2000 and there are plans to repopulate a nearby area with once-indigenous antelope and zebra.

Chimfunshi lacks the resources to accept volunteers. However, visitors with a genuine interest in the work of the orphanage are welcome. A one- or two- week visit is recommended to allow time to get to know the chimps and settle into their daily routine and requirements. Visitors should bear in mind that Chimfunshi's priority is accommodating chimpanzees. Don't expect five-star luxury.

VISITING CHIMFUNSHI

A stay at Chimfunshi Wildlife Orphanage can provide a rewarding insight into the re-habilitation of orphaned, often traumatized, chimpanzees, as well as helping to finance (through accommodation fees) the long process of re-socializing these intelligent creatures. Visitors can spend several hours a day 'minding' baby chimps, as well as studying older ones from a special observation platform. Most of Chimfunshi's chimpanzees are accommodated in three 200ha (500-acre) enclosures which were completed in 2003. It is essential to contact the orphanage well in advance of visiting.

SOUTH TOWARDS LIVINGSTONE

The road from Lusaka to Livingstone is around 470km (290 miles) long and, potholes aside, there are several reasons for the odd diversion.

Highlights

Kafue and Mazabuka, two of the first towns encountered on the journey south, have little of interest to the traveller – unless you are heading for Lechwe Lodge near the former. Further down the road, **Monze** is close to the remains of an old colonial police post called **Fort Monze** and also provides access to **Lochinvar National Park**. A short distance before **Choma** is the turn-off to the **Nkanga River Conservation Area**. Here, you will find activities such as game drives, bush walks, fishing and horse riding. In Choma itself is a fascinating **museum** displaying jewellery, musical instruments, beadwork and other traditional skills of the Tonga people.

Lochinvar National Park ★★★

Stretching 428km² (165 sq miles) across the flood plain of the Kafue River, Lochinvar is an internationally renowned wetland teeming with **birds** and home to an endemic race of antelope known as the **Kafue lechwe**. With splayed hooves and powerful hindquarters to enable them to move freely across waterlogged grasslands, Kafue lechwe number around 30,000 in the national park.

Ideally, keen bird-watchers should visit after the floods when swelling lagoons attract large numbers of waders, ducks and geese. With patience you will soon be ticking off black-tailed godwit, Cape shoveller and pygmy goose among dozens of others. Flocks of wattled crane can also be seen here, along with pelican and flamingo. And if that doesn't have you scrambling for binoculars, Lochinvar's 50 raptor species surely will.

Other highlights include the **Gwisho Hot Springs**, surrounded by graceful ivory palms, and **Drum Rocks** – a strange outcrop that produces a resonating sound when tapped. Nearby is the **Sebanzi Hill**, site of an Iron-Age village. Look out for a large **baobab tree** which has a hollow trunk you could almost contemplate sleeping inside – were it not for the temptation of Lochinvar's luxury tented camp situated near the shores of Chunga Lagoon.

> **BIRD-WATCHING**
>
> Zambia boasts more than 730 species of birds and it is not unusual for individual national parks to have lists exceeding 400 varieties. Prime locations include Lochinvar, South Luangwa and Kasanka national parks. On safari, a pair of binoculars is essential for close-up views of birds and mammals. Choose a lightweight model with X8 or X9 magnification.

Below: *Lochinvar National Park is one of Zambia's premier bird-watching sites.*

Lusaka and Central Zambia at a Glance

BEST TIMES TO VISIT

Lusaka has a pleasant climate with warm summers, mild winters and plenty of sun. **Oct–Nov** can get very hot. Lochinvar National Park is a **year-round** paradise for bird-watchers and photographers.

GETTING THERE

Lusaka
Lusaka is connected to other countries by **air**, **bus**, **rail** and **ferry** (*see* Travel Tips). Transfers between the airport and city centre, about 25km (15 miles), are possible by **taxi** or **hotel courtesy bus**. **Internal flights** connect Lusaka with several destinations, including Chipata, Livingstone, Mfuwe, Mongu and Ndola. **Local buses** and **minibuses** ply the routes to and from Livingstone and the Copperbelt, as well as destinations in east and west Zambia. A **train** connects Lusaka with Livingstone and the Copperbelt. The express service from Livingstone takes 12hr – about twice as long as the bus.
Lochinvar National Park
You can either **drive** yourself (allow at least 2hr) or book a **charter flight**.

GETTING AROUND

Taxis are common in Lusaka. Agree on a price before getting inside – none have meters. It's not really worth **hiring a car** to explore the capital unless you plan to take it further afield and if so, carefully consider a 4x4. Driving on main roads is straight-forward – gravel or sand is another matter. **Buses** leave Lusaka from the main terminal on Dedan Kimathi Road. The **train** station is nearby.

WHERE TO STAY

Lusaka
LUXURY
Hotel InterContinental, Haile Selassie Avenue, PO Box 32201, tel: (01) 250 000, fax: 250 895, e-mail: lusaka@ interconti.com.zm website: www.ichotelsgroup.com Central location, 200 well-equipped rooms, range of restaurants and shops.
Holiday Inn Garden Court Lusaka Ridgeway, Church Road, PO Box 30666, tel: (01) 251 666, fax: 253 529, email: admin@holidayinn. co.zm website: www.ic hotelsgroup.com Central location, large gardens, 117 rooms, pool.
Taj Pamodzi Hotel, Church Road, PO Box 35450, tel: (01) 254 455, fax: 250 995, e-mail: pamodzi.lusaka@taj hotels.com website: www.taj hotels.com Lush gardens, 193 high standard rooms (all with a balcony).

MID-RANGE
Fairview Hotel, Church Road, Postbag E186, tel: (01) 222 604, fax: 237 222, e-mail: fairview@zamnet.zm Friendly, Zambian-owned hotel, *en-suite* rooms.
Endesha Guest House, Parirenyetwa Road, PO Box 32372, tel: (01) 225 780, fax:

225 781. Central, simple and clean, some rooms *en suite*.

BUDGET
Chachacha Backpackers, 161 Mulombwa Close, tel: (01) 222 257. Good value; 10 minutes' walk from city centre.

Nature Reserves and Lodges
LUXURY
Chaminuka Lodge, PO Box 35370, tel: (01) 222 694, e-mail: reservations@ chaminuka.com website: www.chaminuka.com 45km (28 miles) from Lusaka city centre, 18 *en-suite* rooms, comfortable lounges, pool, wildlife-viewing activities. Rustic bush camp nearby.
Lechwe Lodge, PO Box 37940, tel: (01) 704 803, fax: (032) 30707, e-mail: kflechwe@ zamnet.zm, website: www.lechwelodge.com Near Kafue Town, four rondavels, two family chalets, home cooking, pool, game-viewing.
Lilayi Lodge, PO Box 30093, tel: (01) 279 022, fax: 279 026, e-mail: lilayi@zamsaf.co.zm, website: www.lilayi.com 20km (12 miles) south of Lusaka, 12 *en-suite* chalets in parkland, pool, business facilities.
Protea Hotel Lusaka Safari Lodge, 1633 Malambo Road, tel: (01) 212 843, fax: 212 853, e-mail: chisamba@ zamnet.zm website: www.pro teahotels.com 45km (28 miles) north of Lusaka, 20 sumptuous chalets, traditional 'boma-style' restaurant, game-viewing, business facilities, private airstrip.

Lusaka and Central at a Glance

MID-RANGE/BUDGET

Fringilla Lodge, PO Box 1, Fringilla, tel/fax: (01) 213 855, e-mail: fringill@zam net.zm 50km (31 miles) north of Lusaka, camp site, chalets, farm cooking, children's playground.

North towards the Copperbelt
MID-RANGE

Mukwa Guest House, 26/28 Mpezeni Avenue, Kitwe, tel: (02) 224 266, e-mail: trekafrica@coppernet.zm 10 double rooms, swimming pool, car hire and travel agent.
Chimfunshi Wildlife Orphanage, PO Box 11190, Chingola, tel/fax: (02) 311 293, e-mail: chimps@yebo.co.za website: www.chimfunshi. org.za Limited accommo- dation at education centre and camp site.

South towards Livingstone
LUXURY

Lechwe Plains Tented Camp, Lochinvar National Park, Star of Africa, Postnet Box, tel: (01) 271 366, fax: 271 398, e-mail: reservations@starofafrica.co.zw website: www.star-of- africa.com Six double *en-suite* tents, lavish interiors, pool, canoe rides, game drives, angling.

MID-RANGE/BUDGET

Nkanga River Conservation Area, PO Box 630025, Choma, tel/fax: (032) 20592. Lodge with *en-suite* rooms, camp site, game drives, horse riding.

Lusaka's showgrounds have a variety of eateries, including the **Sichuan Chinese Restaurant**. For fast food, head to Cairo Road.

LUXURY/MID-RANGE

Dil Restaurant, 153 Ibex Hill Road, Lusaka, tel: (01) 262 391, fax: 224 515. High quality Indian cuisine.
Le Soleil, Zambezi Road, Roma, tel: (01) 291 801, email: info@lesoleil- zambia.com Peaceful location just outside Lusaka, organic food, health and beauty spa.

MID-RANGE

Café d'Afrique, Lufubu Road, Lusaka, tel: (01) 294 264, e-mail: africafe@zamnet.zm Lunchtime meals; cultural nights with African dishes and traditional dancing and music.
Engineers, Cairo Road, Lusaka, tel: (01) 223 445. Pub atmosphere, light meals, pasta, vegetarian options.
Marlin Restaurant, Lusaka Club, tel: (01) 252 206. Indian, Creole, steaks and more.

Manda Hill Shopping Centre, boutiques and cafés, arcades, various shops, including music stores, plus internet cafés. Bargain for crafts and curios at **Kabwata Cultural Centre** or peruse the paintings and sculp- tures in the city's **art galleries**.

To see Lusaka's highlights simply hop in a taxi or walk. **Adventure City**, Leopards Hill Road, tel: (01) 233 888, swimming pools, water slides, popular with families.
Steve Blagus Travel, 24c Nkwazi Road, tel: (01) 227 739, fax: 225 178, e-mail: sblagus@zamnet.zm
The Zambian Safari Company, Cairo Road, tel: (01) 228 682, fax: 222 906, e-mail: reserva- tions@zamsaf.co.zm

Car hire, Avis, tel: (01) 251 642, New Ace Car Hire, tel: (01) 232 654.
Couriers, DHL, tel: (01) 229 718, Mercury Couriers, tel: (01) 231 137.
Internet Café, Businet, Kabelenga Road, Lusaka.

LUSAKA	J	F	M	A	M	J	J	A	S	O	N	D
AVERAGE TEMP. °F	72	72	72	70	66	63	61	66	72	77	75	72
AVERAGE TEMP. °C	22	22	22	21	19	17	16	19	22	25	24	22
HOURS OF SUN DAILY	6	6	8	10	10	10	10	11	10	10	8	7
RAINFALL in	9	8	6	1	0	0	0	0	0	0.5	4	6
RAINFALL mm	231	191	142	18	3	0	0	0	0	10	91	150
DAYS OF RAINFALL	17	14	10	3	1	0	0	0	0	2	8	16

3
Livingstone and Victoria Falls

Travelling to Zambia and not visiting Victoria Falls is like bypassing Colorado's Grand Canyon or Egypt's pyramids. Not only is it one of the world's most spectacular waterfalls – the Zambezi River crashing 100m (330ft) into a chasm stretching 1.7km (1 mile) in length – but it is also the undisputed adventure capital of southern Africa.

The clouds of spray billowing from Victoria Falls can be seen from as far away as 30km (20 miles). *Mosi-oa-Tunya*, 'The Smoke that Thunders', was how the local Makololo people described it – and explorers were equally spellbound. 'Scenes so lovely must have been gazed upon by angels in their flight,' wrote Dr David Livingstone when, in 1855, he became the first European to explore the area around the Falls.

Nowadays, you can **fly like an angel** over Victoria Falls – courtesy of an aircraft, helicopter, microlight, hot-air balloon or parachute. You can take a leap of faith from the Victoria Falls Bridge on one of the world's highest **bungee jumps**. You can **raft rapids** in the zigzagging chasm downstream of the Falls, known as Batoka Gorge, or **canoe** calmer stretches of the Upper Zambezi.

But Victoria Falls is not solely the realm of adrenaline addicts. **Livingstone** offers an intriguing glimpse into the region's colonial past. There are several **cultural and craft centres** as well as **museums** on both the Zambian side of Victoria Falls and in the Zimbabwean town of the same name. For wildlife enthusiasts, **Mosi-oa-Tunya** and **Zambezi national parks** support a variety of species, including elephant, buffalo and giraffe.

DON'T MISS

*** Victoria Falls: admire this World Heritage Site from a series of viewpoints.
*** Whitewater rafting: shoot the awesome rapids in Batoka Gorge.
*** The Upper Zambezi: canoe tranquil waters past herds of elephant, or stay at a luxurious riverside lodge.
** Livingstone: investigate Zambia's colonial capital at the museum, then shop for crafts and curios.
** Mosi-oa-Tunya National Park: spot Zambia's only white rhino.

Opposite: Mosi-oa-Tunya, *the Smoke that Thunders.*

Above: *Only from the air can the true scale of Victoria Falls be fully appreciated.*

HISTORY

Long before Dr Livingstone had even heard of a great waterfall slicing across the Zambezi, the local people already had a name for it. Literally meaning 'smoke does sound there', *Mosi-oa-Tunya* vividly portrayed the awe with which the Makololo viewed the rumbling clouds of spray that rose above this natural wonder. Even so, when Livingstone journeyed downstream to see the Falls for himself, he had already renamed them in honour of his queen.

Although the Makololo rarely ventured close to Victoria Falls, the Scottish missionary and explorer managed to find men familiar enough with the Zambezi's rapids to take him to the very brink of the cataract.

'[They] brought me to an island situated in the middle of the river, on the edge of the lip over which the water rolls,' recorded Livingstone. 'Creeping with awe to the verge, I peered down into a large rent which had been made from bank to bank of the broad Zambezi, and saw that a stream of a thousand yards broad leaped down a hundred feet and then became suddenly compressed into a space of fifteen to twenty yards... the most wonderful sight I had witnessed in Africa.'

In the years that followed Livingstone's 'discovery', Victoria Falls became a magnet to other travellers. In 1881, Frederick Selous' description positively gushed with enthusiasm when he described the Falls as 'one of the most transcendentally beautiful natural phenomena on this side of Paradise.'

By the end of the 19th century, traders, missionaries and hunters had settled at **Old Drift**, a ferry crossing about 10km (6 miles) upstream of the Falls. A small cemetery marking the site can still be seen in Mosi-oa-Tunya National Park.

Old Drift seemed a natural choice for a settlement – the Victoria Falls was the most easterly point people could travel by boat along the Upper Zambezi. But malarial mosquitoes plagued the early settlers. In 1905, when the newly completed Victoria Falls Bridge (commissioned by Cecil Rhodes) provided a rail link across the Zambezi, they moved to a healthier location called Constitution Hill which was near the railway line. Six years later, this small community, known as **Livingstone**, became the capital of what was then Northern Rhodesia. Many of its original colonial buildings still stand in the town centre.

Inevitably, the railway line brought the first wave of tourists to Victoria Falls. On the southern side of the Zambezi River in Rhodesia (now Zimbabwe), work began on constructing the **Victoria Falls Hotel** – initially a modest affair of wood and corrugated iron. In 1914 it was replaced by a more comfortable brick building. There was even a track laid nearby to convey pampered guests to the Falls in trolleys pushed by servants.

Luxury is still a benchmark of the elegant, Edwardian-style hotel with its manicured lawns and fine views of the bridge and gorges downstream of Victoria Falls. Nowadays, however, the plethora of tourists visiting Livingstone and Victoria Falls each year can take advantage of a bewildering array of accommodation and activities. Needless to say, the star attraction remains the Falls themselves. After all, what could possibly steal the thunder of *Mosi-oa-Tunya*?

Below: *Set in pristine gardens on the Zimbabwean side of the River Zambezi, Victoria Falls Hotel offers colonial-style splendour.*

VICTORIA FALLS GEOLOGY

1. Basalt lava seeps across western Zambia 150 million years ago.
2. The lava cools and cracks.
3. Tectonic activity lifts the basalt to form a plateau.
4. One million years ago the Zambezi and Matetsi rivers flow either side of the plateau.
5. Earth movements force the Zambezi north where it plunges over the edge of a huge rift in the plateau.
6. The river exploits the cracks in the basalt, creating a new waterfall at each one and forming the distinctive zigzag outline of Batoka Gorge.
7. The present-day Victoria Falls is the eighth waterfall in this succession. A new fracture being eroded at Devil's Cataract indicates that it won't be the last.

LIVINGSTONE

Located just 10km (6 miles) north of Victoria Falls, Livingstone is Zambia's most popular tourist centre. A compact town, centred around the railway line and Mosi-oa-Tunya Road, Livingstone is experiencing a boom in tourism and now offers a great variety of places to stay. The town has lots of historical and cultural interest and is also the gateway to prime stretches of the Upper Zambezi, not to mention unique perspectives of the Falls themselves.

Museums **

The **Livingstone Museum**, adjacent to the Tourist Office on Mosi-oa-Tunya Road, is perhaps the most interesting of Livingstone's three museums. The broad range of archaeological and anthropological exhibits includes some of Dr David Livingstone's original journals and letters. There are also indigenous ritual artefacts and weapons, historical African maps, as well as a replica of the 125,000-year-old human skull excavated near Kabwe, north of Lusaka. Near the entrance, a large relief map of the Victoria Falls region helps to put everything in perspective. Open daily 09:00–16:30. The **Railway Museum** (also known as the Zambezi Sawmills Locomotive Sheds National Monument) lies on the town's southern outskirts. For railway buffs, it's an historical treasure full of rusting old engines, rolling stock and other memorabilia. For non-enthusiasts it's an historical treasure full of rust! Open daily, 08:30–16:00.

Beyond Livingstone, near the Falls, is the small **Field Museum** which is located on the site of an archaeological dig. Prehistoric artefacts up to three million years old were found here, along with tools that suggest Stone-Age people inhabited the area at least 50,000 years ago. Other excavations point to the presence of hunter-gatherer communities until as recently as 2000 years ago.

Local Culture ★★

Zambia's rich cultural heritage can be experienced through art, music, dance and food at the **Maramba Cultural Village**. Located next to the Livingstone Showgrounds and opened in early 2007, the village consists of an art gallery, nine model villages and an open air theatre with a seating capacity of 450.

Tour operators in Livingstone can also arrange visits to the **Mukuni Village** east of the Falls where a local guide will provide insights into the daily lives of this typical settlement of 7000 people. Each February, the local Leya people make offerings to ancestral spirits whom they believe still dwell in Batoka Gorge.

The best local market in Livingstone is **Maramba Market** which sells everything from fruit and vegetables to local fabrics.

Shopping for Crafts and Curios ★★

Livingstone will satiate even the most ardent souvenir-hunter. Not only is there a good range of craft centres and curio stalls, but bargain-seekers will generally find prices much cheaper than in Zimbabwe. Although vendors are fully prepared for bargaining, remember that this is their livelihood – haggle hard, but fairly. Many carvings are made from increasingly rare African hardwoods, so it's also important to take environmental ethics into consideration. Finally, bear in mind that not everything is produced locally. Some of the curios may come from as far afield as West Africa.

Above: *Local women prepare frothy beer, called 'shake-shake', at Maramba Market.*
Opposite: *The Livingstone Museum houses a large collection of David Livingstone memorabilia.*

RAILWAY MUSEUM

Historic trains and vintage coaches at Livingstone's Railway Museum include the Pioneer Rhodesia 7th-class steam locomotive, the Mine Hunslet steam locomotive, and the Cape Government Railways 7th-class steam locomotives that date from the 1890s. The Museum also contains records of the more recent Tanzania-Zambia Railway (TAZARA) and there is a shop selling souvenirs and books.

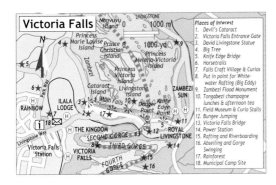

Victoria Falls

Places of Interest
1. Devil's Cataract
2. Victoria Falls Entrance Gate
3. David Livingstone Statue
4. Big Tree
5. Knife Edge Bridge
6. Horsetrails
7. Falls Craft Village & Curios
8. Put in point for Whitewater Rafting (Big Eddy)
9. Zambezi Flood Monument
10. Tongabezi champagne
    lunches & afternoon tea
11. Field Museum & Curio Stalls
12. Bungee Jumping
13. Victoria Falls Bridge
14. Power Station
15. Rafting and Riverboarding
16. Abseiling and Gorge
    Swinging
17. Rainforest
18. Municipal Camp Site

If you have the time and tenacity for bartering, look no further than the curio stalls near the **Field Museum**. Here you will find a kaleidoscope of crafts, from spindly wooden giraffes and malachite chess boards to woven baskets and soapstone paperweights. A similar array of curios can be found at the **Curio and Craft Centre** in Livingstone's Mukuni Park. For more relaxed browsing, head to one of the town's art and craft shops. The **Livingstone Museum** has a small shop selling good value baskets. More upmarket are **Kubu Crafts** and **African Visions** which, in addition to carvings and baskets, stock more unusual items such as jewellery, pottery, furniture and artefacts.

VICTORIA FALLS

Over 100m (330ft) tall, 1.7km (1 mile) in length, 550 million litres (23 million gallons) of water pouring over the edge every minute – Victoria Falls boasts impressive credentials. But nothing can prepare visitors for their first close-up view of this UNESCO World Heritage Site. Soaked by mist, the ground trembling beneath their feet, it is both humbling and exciting to walk within metres of the tempests of spray and plumes of roaring white water; the Zambezi dashed violently on basalt rocks while rainbows arch overhead. Viewing Victoria Falls is, quite simply, the experience of a lifetime.

Viewing the Falls ★★★

Viewing the Falls from both the Zambian and Zimbabwean sides is straightforward and perfectly safe – as long as you don't stray too near the edge. Islands perched on the lip of the Falls have divided them into several cataracts which, starting from the Zambian side, are Eastern Cataract, Armchair Falls, Rainbow Falls, Horseshoe Falls, Main Falls and Devil's Cataract.

THE BRIDGE

Spanning the gorge a short distance downstream of Victoria Falls, the dramatic steel bridge over the Zambezi was constructed in the early 1900s. Designed by Sir Douglas Fox and manufactured in England, the single-arch, cantilevered bridge was located so that spray from the Falls would land on the carriages and cool its passengers. However, when engineers came to assemble it, the final piece refused to fit. Seemingly, they had not taken into account the expansive effect of a hot African sun. Early the next morning the bridge slotted perfectly into place.

When walking to the various viewpoints, remember to wear shoes with good grips (paths and steps may be slippery from the spray), take a light raincoat or poncho and pack cameras in moisture-proof bags.

The Zambian Side

Three walking routes begin near the Field Museum. The most spectacular crosses spindly **Knife Edge Bridge** to a panoramic viewpoint of Eastern Cataract. Another descends to the water's edge at the **Boiling Pot**, a very steep climb, but worthwhile in order to witness the Zambezi squeezed into the narrow defile of Batoka Gorge. A third path leads **upstream**, providing glimpses of the smooth expanse of the Upper Zambezi moments before it plummets into the void.

Towards the end of the dry season, a fourth option may be possible. Occasionally, the channels of the Zambezi dry out sufficiently to enable people to walk as far as **Livingstone Island**, where the famous explorer is believed to have first peered over the edge. Perched on the very lip of the Falls, this wooded islet provides a unique and giddy perspective. Tongabezi Lodge, located further upstream, can arrange breakfast, champagne lunch or afternoon tea and cocktails on the island between July and March.

Below: *A close-up of Victoria Falls Bridge reveals the platform from which bungee jumpers leap into Batoka Gorge.*

BEST VIEWPOINTS

- **Cataract View** for a spray-drenched view along the Falls from within the gorge itself.
- **Danger Point** for a classic panorama.
- **Knife Edge Bridge** for an exciting view of the Eastern Cataracts.
- **Livingstone Island** for a unique, ground-trembling perspective from the very lip of the Falls.
- **Flight of the Angels** (either from a helicopter, light aircraft, microlight or ultralight) to appreciate the full scale of the natural wonder.

Below: *For many people, this pool on Livingstone Island, perched on the lip of the Falls, is a little too close for comfort.*

The Zimbabwean Side

Viewing the Falls is more regulated south of the Zambezi. A fee is payable at the entrance to **Victoria Falls National Park**, after which you can wander the network of trails on your own. Start at the westernmost point where there is a stoic-looking **statue of Dr Livingstone**, inscribed with the words 'Explorer, Missionary and Liberator'. Nearby, a steep, and often slippery, stone stairway descends through dripping vegetation into the chasm of Victoria Falls. Senses take a pummelling when you reach **Cataract View** at the base of the stairs, with its awesome views along the length of the Falls.

Climbing back towards Livingstone's statue, there is a choice of trails. Turn right to follow a path alongside the Zambezi where you may glimpse a variety of animals, including hippos and crocodiles. Do not be tempted to go for a swim! After around 2km (1.25 miles) the trail reaches **The Big Tree**, a giant baobab which once served as a camp site for early settlers waiting to cross the river to Old Drift.

The left-hand path from Livingstone's statue leads directly in front of Victoria Falls, threading through a unique **rainforest** sustained by the constant spray. It is a fragile ecosystem, home to rare plants, such as ebony, ivory palm, African olive, strangler fig and many types of fern. Shy bushbuck are sometimes seen here, while vigilant bird-watchers may spot Taita falcons, black storks, black eagles and augur buzzards – all of which nest in the gorges downstream.

At frequent intervals, loops in the trail lead to viewpoints opposite the Falls. Don't rush! Not only are the barriers scant or non-existent, but the spray and sunlight conditions are constantly changing,

providing a beautiful sequence of rainbows and light effects.

The trail ends at **Danger Point**, a popular place to watch the spray turn gold at sunset. Returning to the park entrance gate, a small detour leads to a clearing from which views of Victoria Falls Bridge and the screaming antics of bungee jumpers can be quite entertaining.

Victoria Falls Town ★★

The Zimbabwean town of Victoria Falls is less than 2km (1.25 miles) south of the Zambezi. Unlike Livingstone, it is within easy walking distance of the Falls. A major crossroads for travellers, Victoria Falls has excellent hotels, restaurants, shops and tour operators. Political unrest in Zimbabwe hasn't helped the town's tourism – just as Livingstone's tourism booom has tempted many visitors to the Zambian side of the Falls.

There is no denying, however, that Victoria Falls can cater to just about every tourist whim – whether it's an action-packed day on the river or a game drive in nearby **Zambezi National Park**. Needless to say, shoppers are well catered for at the **Victoria Falls Craft Village** on Livingstone Way, as well as the **Elephant's Walk Shopping Complex**.

No visit to Victoria Falls would be complete without sampling the excellent cuisine of the historical **Victoria Falls Hotel**. If the formal attire required for dinner in the Livingstone Room is off-putting, try instead the more casual buffet breakfast or their delicious afternoon tea served on the sun terrace.

Above: *Visitors gather at Danger Point to watch the sunset over Victoria Falls.*

ZIMBABWE FACT FILE

Independence: 1980.
Total Area: 390,757km²
(150,832 sq miles).
Capital: Harare.
Population: 13 million.
Time Zone: GMT+2.
International Dialling Code: 263.
Language: officially English, but with Shona and Ndebele dialects also spoken.
Religion: Christian, Muslim, Hindu, Jewish and traditional African beliefs.
Currency: Zimbabwe dollar.
Industry: agriculture, livestock, mining, manufacturing.

ACTIVITIES

'Come to the edge – we'll take you beyond.' That is how one adventure tour operator tempts visitors to sample the extraordinary array of activities available at Victoria Falls. Don't worry, however, if you find the prospect of whitewater rafting or bungee jumping anything but tempting. Activities at the Falls cater to all levels of adrenaline abuse, from a gentle sundowner cruise on the Upper Zambezi or a ride on a steam train to surfing the rapids on a body board or bungee jumping into a waiting raft – the so-called 'gruesome twosome.'

Flight of the Angels ★★★

Although some visitors bemoan the frequent buzz of helicopters and light aircraft above the Falls, this is still the best way to fully appreciate their awesome scale. A breathtaking aerial perspective of Victoria Falls can be achieved in a number of ways. The most novel perhaps is to fly above them in a vintage **de Havilland Tiger Moth biplane** with open cockpits. An alternative that doesn't involve a noisy engine is to bale out of a plane with a **parachute**. If that sounds a little extreme, however, there are regular scenic flights available using either a **helicopter** or **light aircraft**.

A typical 15-minute Flight of the Angels will include a few circuits over the Falls (clockwise and anticlockwise to ensure everyone gets a good view), followed by a brief foray upstream to spot hippos and elephants along the Upper Zambezi. Longer 30-minute flights involve more laps around the Falls and aerial game-spotting over Zambezi National Park. Helicopter charter flights are also possible, perhaps incorporating an island champagne lunch or a pick-up following a whitewater rafting trip.

TAKE TO THE SKIES

Flight of the Angels trips can be booked through:
Batoka Sky, Maramba Aerodrome, Livingstone, tel: (03) 320 058, fax: 324 071, e-mail: freedom@zamnet.zm, website: www.batokasky.com Daily scenic flights in fixed-wing Cessnas, helicopters and microlights.
Zambezi Helicopter Company, Shearwater Adventures (see page 61). Daily scenic helicopter flights.
Bush Birds Flying Safaris, Victoria Falls Airport, tel: (26313) 43398, fax: 42411. Ultralight flights.
Tandemania, Soper's Arcade, Victoria Falls, tel/fax: (011) 211 092. Tandem parachute jumps.
United Air Charter, Livingstone International Airport, tel: (03) 323 095, fax: (03) 322 620, email: uac@microlink.zam, website: www.uaczam.com. Flights in helicopters and a 1931 Tiger Moth biplane.

The photographic potential of the Flight of the Angels is superb. Remember to take plenty of spare film and keep the camera as close to the window as possible to avoid interior reflections spoiling the picture. Keen photographers with a sense of adventure should seriously consider a flight in an **ultralight**. These small light aircraft, with room for just the pilot and one passenger, have open cockpits allowing the ultimate aerial experience of the Falls. **Microlights** are similar, but due to the proximity of the propeller, cameras cannot be carried. Instead, the operators will mount a camera on the wing for that special souvenir snapshot.

Whitewater Rafting ★★★

Admittedly, the names can be unnerving. Oblivion, Terminator, The Devil's Toilet Bowl and Gnashing Jaws of Death are just a few of the rapids located in Batoka Gorge downstream of Victoria Falls. Although world renowned, whitewater rafting on this stretch of the Zambezi has been described as 'extremely difficult, with long and violent rapids, steep gradients, big drops and pressure areas.' Obviously, it is not for the faint-hearted. However, with operators adhering to strict safety standards, whitewater rafting has deservedly become one of the Falls' most popular activities.

TAKING THE PLUNGE

Whitewater rafting trips can be booked through:
Adrift, PO Box 233, Victoria Falls, tel: (26313) 4502, e-mail: rafting@adrift.co.uk, website: www.adrift.co.uk Highly experienced operator, licensed to start at rapids near the base of the Falls. **Bundu Adventures**, PO Box 60773, Livingstone, tel: (03) 324 407, e-mail: zambezi@zamnet.zm website: www.bundu adventures.com Large, experienced company offering rafting, riverboarding and canoeing.
Safari Par Excellence (see page 61)
Jet boat tours can be booked through **Jet Extreme**, Shearwater Adventures (see page 61). Another large operator offering full range of activities.
Touch Adventure, 2586 Chitimukulu Road, tel: (03) 321 111, email: raft@touch adventure.com, website: www.touchadventure.com. Rafting company established in 2000.

Opposite: *Markets at Victoria Falls provide a wide range of curios.*
Left: *Open to the elements, a microlight is a stimulating way to view the Falls.*

LOW OR HIGH WATER

Whitewater rafting trips take place in low water (Aug–Jan) or high water (Feb–Jul). **Low water** trips start in the Boiling Pot. The first major rapid is Morning Glory, followed by Stairway to Heaven (involving a steep drop) and The Devil's Toilet Bowl (grade 4). Next is Gulliver's Travels (achieving the ultimate grade 5) and Star Trekking (grade 4). Everyone portages Commerical Suicide (grade 6) before enjoying Gnashing Jaws of Death, a grade 3 'wave train'. **High water** trips usually start at Overland Truck Eater (rapid 11), followed by The Mother and a nerve-jangling 700m (2300ft) stretch of white water known as Terminator (grade 4 or 5). Double Trouble and Oblivion (both grade 4), followed by several grade 3 rapids, complete the day.

A typical day's rafting begins with a land-based briefing and the issuing of lifejackets, helmets and paddles (and wetsuit tops during the colder months between April and August). Rafters then trek down a steep path to the bottom of the gorge where the inflatable rubber rafts are waiting. The prevailing water levels determine the starting point – some rapids may be avoided during dangerous low water periods.

Training begins in a calm stretch with highly experienced skippers coaching their crews of eight on the essentials of whitewater rafting. This includes paddling technique, what to do if the raft capsizes and how to get back in again. Usually, this is accompanied by a torrent of 'raft-speak' – terms like 'flips', 'high-riding' and 'downtime' may sound technical, but they generally involve being tossed violently from the raft into the kind of water most people have only experienced from the safe side of a washing machine set to fast-rinse.

Many of the rapids are graded IV and V (VI is considered commercially impossible). They are separated by long calm stretches, allowing time to contemplate the dramatic gorge scenery. Safety kayakers always shoot the rapids first and wait downstream ready to assist people

who inadvertently find themselves taking a swim.

Typically, about 24km (15 miles) can be rafted during a day trip, but some operators offer **multi-day options**, camping overnight on riverside beaches. If rafting sounds too tame, try **river-boarding** where the mighty Zambezi can be confronted with nothing more than a small float and a pair of flippers. It is an exhilarating experience to surf the rapids' perpetual breakers, and there is always a back-up raft present if your nerve fails.

Jet Boating ★★

Reaching speeds of over 90km/h (55mph), jet boats also operate in Batoka Gorge, skimming over

rapids and spinning on flat water as they career past the sheer walls. There is no doubting the exhilaration factor of these rides, but some may feel that they compromise the natural sights and sounds of Victoria Falls' gorges.

Bungee Jumping ★★

Spanning no-man's-land between the border posts of Zambia and Zimbabwe, the Victoria Falls Bridge has become a Mecca to thousands of people in search of the ultimate adrenaline rush. With a drop of 111m (364ft), it is one of the highest bungee jump sites in the world.

Registration and safety briefings take place on the Zambian side of the bridge. The maximum weight per jumper is 140kg (309 pounds) and the minimum age is 14. Do not even contemplate jumping if you are pregnant

Above: *On some trips, everyone has a paddle, while on others the skipper takes control with a pair of oars.*
Opposite: *Whitewater rafting is justifiably popular in the churning rapids downstream of Victoria Falls.*

or suffer from high blood pressure, heart conditions, epilepsy, or back or leg injuries.

The standard jump is disconcertingly straightforward! You wear a full body harness, an elastic cord is tied around your ankles and then you simply step off the bridge with the words '5-4-3-2-1-Bungee!' ringing in your ears.

Of course, standard jumps have long since been eclipsed by a daredevil range of embellishments. There are now star elevators, shooting stars, back dives and tandems – some of which are self-explanatory, while others are almost beyond belief.

For a slower descent into the gorge, **abseiling** is also available – although even this can be enhanced by a 'gorge swing' which involves free-falling off a cliff for 50m (165ft) before being swung like a pendulum into the middle of the chasm.

Upper Zambezi Canoeing ★★★

Although there are a few minor rapids, activities upstream of the Falls focus on a more sedate appreciation of the scenery and wildlife. Inflatable two-person canoes are used for a typical day's paddling covering about 25km (15 miles) of the Upper Zambezi. It is an excellent opportunity to drift silently past the diverse wildlife of the Zambezi National Park.

Elephant, giraffe, waterbuck and other varieties of antelope often come down to the water's edge to drink. The bird life is equally prolific. Bee-eaters excavate nesting colonies in the sandy river banks, while herons, kingfishers, hamerkops, African fish eagles and other water-loving species are frequently sighted. Hippos are common too, but they tend to be territorial and your guides will know how to avoid them.

STEP FORWARD

Bungee jumping at Victoria Falls is organized by **African Extreme**, PO Box 60233, Livingstone, tel: (03) 324 156, email: bungee@zamnet.zm, www.shearwateradventures.com

For gorge swinging, abseiling, rap jumping and highwiring, contact: **The Zambezi Swing**, PO Box 61023, Livingstone, tel: (03) 321 188, email: theswing@zamnet.zm, website: www.thezambeziswing.com

A two- or three-day canoe trip is the perfect way to explore the Upper Zambezi and visit many of its islands. Several lodges on the Zambian side of the river offer luxurious accommodation, while some islands, like Sindabezi, have simple thatched camps and offer outstanding bird-watching opportunities.

River Cruises ★★
Various vessels operate cruises on the Upper Zambezi River. The popular sundowner option (commonly referred to as the 'booze cruise') usually lasts around three hours. Other cruises coincide with breakfast, lunch or afternoon tea and, although they offer a less intimate wildlife experience than canoeing, there is still a good chance of spotting common species like hippos and crocodiles.

Fishing trips can be arranged on the Upper Zambezi and in Batoka Gorge below the Falls. The best time for catching tiger fish is August to March.

Train Rides ★
Departing from Livingstone Station, the Victoria Falls Safari Express steam train takes passengers on the short run to Victoria Falls Bridge where it pauses for a photo opportunity before returning again.

Elephant Riding ★★
Operating from Thorntree River Lodge, Livingstone, African elephants have been trained to carry tourists on short safaris. As well as teaching you about the elephants' behaviour and conservation issues, these unusual safaris offer a good chance of spotting birds and other wildlife.

Opposite: For the ultimate adrenaline rush, few activities can compete with bungee jumping.
Below: In contrast, riverboat cruises on the Upper Zambezi are calm and sedate.

Horse Riding **

Horse-riding safaris operate on both sides of the river. Novices can learn the basics during half-day sessions, while the more experienced riders can set off into the bush on overnight safari adventures.

Quad Biking **

An excellent way in which to explore the spectacular landscape around Livingstone and the Batoka Gorge, all-terrain quad bikes are suitable for both novice and experienced riders.

NATIONAL PARKS

There are three national parks in the immediate vicinity of Victoria Falls – Mosi-oa-Tunya in Zambia and both the Zambezi and Victoria Falls national parks in Zimbabwe. Most, if not all, visitors experience Victoria Falls National Park with its incredible close-up views of the cataracts. Mosi-oa-Tunya National Park encloses the eastern section of the Falls and several of the gorges downstream, but this reserve, together with Zambezi National Park, also offers excellent game-viewing along the Upper Zambezi and adjacent land.

Mosi-oa-Tunya National Park ***

Covering 67km² (26 sq miles), only a small section of Mosi-oa-Tunya is fenced off into a game park. Nevertheless, it is well worth a visit, having to go on your own or going on an organized safari. One of the highlights include five white rhino which are probably found nowhere else in Zambia and are usually being trailed by their personal guard.

The predominant vegetation is mopane forest with small areas of teak and miombo woodland. Giraffe, eland, wildebeest, impala, warthog, baboon and vervet monkey are all commonly seen – as are elephant which migrate across the Zambezi during the dry season.

Zambezi National Park ★★★

With 40km (25 miles) of river frontage, Zambezi National Park extends south in a wildlife-rich mosaic of mopane forest and savanna. The park covers an area of 348km^2 (216 sq miles) and supports large numbers of elephant, buffalo, zebra and giraffe, as well as some magnificent sable antelope. Predators, such as lion and African wild dog, are also present.

In addition to canoe trips on the Zambezi River, wildlife-watching in the park is possible on game drives operating from the town of Victoria Falls.

SAFARIS FURTHER AFIELD

If you are staying in the Victoria Falls area for any length of time, there are several excellent national parks within reach of a short safari. **Kafue National Park** can be visited by charter flight from Livingstone, while two reliable options outside Zambia include Zimbabwe's **Hwange National Park** and Botswana's **Chobe National Park**. Hwange, covering an area of 14,650km^2 (5650 sq miles), has large herds of elephant, buffalo, zebra and antelope and provides particularly good game-viewing from Sep–Oct when animals gather around water holes. Chobe encompasses 11,000km^2 (4250 sq miles) of varied and wildlife-rich habitats, including the magnificent Linyanti and Savuti Marshes.

Opposite: *Elephant-back safaris provide a unique perspective of the African bush.*
Left: *Zambia's national bird, the African fish eagle, is commonly seen and heard near lakes and rivers.*

Livingstone and Victoria Falls at a Glance

Victoria Falls are impressive year-round. When the Zambezi reaches peak flood (**Mar–Apr**), the clouds of spray look spectacular from the air, but close-up views on foot are often obscured. Views improve in later months until the low water period, (**Sep–Nov**), when the cataracts dwindle and it's possible to raft to the base of the Falls or walk to Livingstone Island. When the river is low, 23 rapids in Batoka Gorge can be rafted. During high water (**Feb–Jul**), only the last 13 rapids are navigable.

Livingstone

There are regular **flights** from Lusaka, as well as daily **buses** and **minibuses**. The Zambezi Express **train** operates between Livingstone and the capital three times weekly.

Victoria Falls, Zimbabwe

20km (12.5 miles) south of the town, Victoria Falls airport handles **flights** from neighbouring countries and from within Zimbabwe. Regular **buses** and an overnight **steam train** connect with Bulawayo, while **long-distance buses** go from Victoria Falls to Windhoek and Cape Town.

Livingstone

Located 10km (6 miles) south of Livingstone, the Falls are easily reached by **taxi**, **bus** or **hire car**. **Bikes** can also be hired.

You will need your passport to cross the border to and from Zimbabwe. Be sure to check visa requirements.

Victoria Falls, Zimbabwe

Taxis and hotel **courtesy buses** operate between the airport and town which, once you've arrived, is within easy **walking** distance of the Falls.

Livingstone

LUXURY

The Royal Livingstone, Mosi-oa-Tunya Road, tel: (03) 321 122, fax: 321 128, website: www.suninternational.co.za 5-star resort with 173 rooms. On the banks of the Zambezi, just upstream from the Falls.

MID-RANGE

New Fairmount Hotel, between Mose and Mwela streets, tel: (03) 320 723, fax: 321 490, email: nfhc@zam net.zm, central location, good facilities.

Songwe Village, c/o Kwando Safaris, website: www.kwando. co.za, spectacular location above Batoka Gorge, 8 thatched huts in traditional village layout.

Zambezi Sun, Mosi-oa-Tunya Road, colourful, 212-room 3 star sibling of the Royal Livingstone (*see* above), great for families.

BUDGET

Fawlty Towers International Backpackers, PO Box 61170, 216 Mosi-oa-Tunya Road, tel/fax: (03) 323 432, e-mail: ahorizon@zamnet.zm

Camping, clean basic rooms, swimming pool, Hippo's Bar & Restaurant, bike hire, booking office for activities.

Victoria Falls, Zimbabwe

LUXURY

Victoria Falls Hotel, PO Box 10, Mallett Drive, tel: (26313) 44751 or 44203, fax: 44762, e-mail: reservations@tvfh. zimsun.co.zw website: www.victoriafallshotel.com World renowned, superb views, fine dining.

MID-RANGE

Ilala Lodge, PO Box 18, tel: (26313) 44203. Central location, pool and gardens.

Upper Zambezi

LUXURY

Sussi & Chuma, Star of Africa, *see* page 41. Ten romantic tree houses, pool.

Tongabezi Lodge, Postbag 31, tel: (03) 324 450, e-mail: reservations@ tongabezi.com website: www.tongabezi.com Riverside suites and cottages, swimming 'rock pool', thatched camp on Sindabezi Island, Tangala family house.

The River Club, book through Wilderness Safaris, website: www.wilderness-safaris.com Open-fronted colonial-style cottages overlooking river.

BUDGET

Jungle Junction, Mosi-oa-Tunya Road, Livingstone, tel: (03) 323 708, e-mail: jungle@zamnet.zm Camp site, huts, a shop and a bar on an island.

Livingstone and Victoria Falls at a Glance

Livingstone
LUXURY
The Royal Livingstone, *see*
left. Superb food and service,
elegant setting.
MID-RANGE
Funky Monkey, 214 Mosi-oa-
Tunya Road, Good for steaks.
The Zambezi Waterfront,
Sichango Road, *see* Safari Par
Excellence below. Good value
and variety, riverside location.

Victoria Falls, Zimbabwe
LUXURY
Victoria Falls Hotel, *see* left.
Formal à la carte menu, after-
noon tea served on terrace.
MID-RANGE
Boma Restaurant, Victoria Falls
Safari Lodge, PO Box 29,
tel: (26313) 43201, fax: 43205,
e-mail: saflodge@saflodge.
co.zw website: www.vfsl.com
Game meats, local food.

General Operators
Safari Par Excellence, PO Box
CT20, Victoria Falls, tel:
(26313) 44424, fax: 44510,
e-mail: ziminfo@safpar.com
or write to PO Box 6490,
Livingstone, tel: (03) 321 629,
fax: 326 629, e-mail: zaminfo@
safpar.com website: www.saf
par.com Full range of activities from elephant-back
safaris to canoeing.
Shearwater Adventures,
Park Way, Victoria Falls,
tel: (26313) 44471, email:
reservations@shearwater.co.zw
website: www.shearwater
adventures.com

Large company operating
most adventures.

Flight of the Angels, see page
52.

*Whitewater Rafting & Jet
Boating, see* page 53.

Abseiling and Bungee Jumping,
see page 56.

Upper Zambezi Canoeing
Makora Quest, PO Box 60420,
Livingstone, tel: (03) 324 253,
e-mail: safari@zamnet.zm
Established Zambian operator.
**Chundukwa Adventure
Trails**, PO Box 61025,
Livingstone, tel: (03) 324 452,
e-mail: chundukwa@zamnet.
zm Horse trails from 1–5
hours to 2 days along the
banks of the Upper Zambezi.

River Cruises
**African Princess Cruise
Company**, PO Box 60733,
Livingstone, tel: (03) 321 513,
fax: 324 070, email: african.
queen@thevictoriafalls.co.zm
Lunch, dinner and sunset
cruises on the African Queen.
Bwaato Adventures, Post
Office complex, Livingstone,
tel: (03) 324 227, fax: 321 490.
River cruises, safaris in Mosi-
oa-Tunya National Park.

Victoria Falls River Safaris, PO
Box 61109, Livingstone, tel/fax:
(03) 321 513, e-mail: river
safaris@thevictoriafalls.co.zm,
website: www.vicfallsriver
safaris.com Small-group
safaris, specially silenced boats.

Train Rides
Victoria Falls Safari Express,
groups only (min 10 pax) book
through Safari Par Excellence
(*see* left).

Elephant Riding
Book through Safari Pow
Excellen Excellence (*see* left).
Half-day elephant-back safaris
in Mosi-oa-Tunya.

Horse Riding
Safari Pow Excellence, Wildlife
Africa, 129A Kitson Street,
Waterval Estate, Northcliff 2195,
South Africa 2195, tel/fax: (27
11) 782 3410, e-mail:
info@wildafrica.co.za Half-
to 3-day trips for experienced
riders, 3hr novice sessions.
Kalai Safaris, *see* page 58.

*Safaris and Local Sightseeing
Tours*
National Tourist Board Tourist
Office, Mosi-oa-Tunya Road,
Livingstone, tel: (03) 321 404,
fax: 321 487.

LIVINGSTONE	J	F	M	A	M	J	J	A	S	O	N	D
AVERAGE TEMP. °F	77	77	75	73	66	63	61	66	75	79	79	77
AVERAGE TEMP. °C	25	25	24	23	19	17	16	19	24	26	26	25
RAINFALL in	7	6	3	1	0	0	0	0	0	1	3	4
RAINFALL mm	174	141	80	24	6	1	0	1	2	25	70	109

4
The Lower Zambezi
and Lake Kariba

Close encounters with large herds of elephant; canoeing at dusk along river channels sparkling with fireflies; listening to the haunting cry of the African fish eagle – these are just some of the experiences awaiting visitors to **Lower Zambezi National Park**.

This beautiful reserve, with fine woodland and abundant wildlife, fringes the northern bank of the Zambezi River as it meanders across a broad rift valley lined by escarpments reaching 1200m (3940ft) in height. **Canoeing** on the river is a highlight of any visit. However, with around 350 bird species, prolific elephant, buffalo and hippo, plus a healthy lion population, traditional vehicle **safaris** in the park can be just as rewarding.

The second main attraction along this stretch of the Zambezi is also spectacular. Anyone who has witnessed the unbridled power of Victoria Falls may find it inconceivable that the Zambezi River could ever be tamed. However, some 160km (100 miles) downstream of the Falls, Africa's fourth longest river flows into a vast artificial lake created by one of the world's largest dams. **Lake Kariba** covers an area of 5200km^2 (2000 sq miles). It has a storage capacity of 180km^3 – all restrained by the curving concrete wall of **Kariba Dam**.

Notwithstanding various controversies during its construction in the late 1950s, the dam has created a valuable **fishing** industry and a mini-boom in **water sports** – not to mention a source of hydroelectric power for Zambia and Zimbabwe. A few small **islands**, once hilltops before the valley was flooded, are now important nature sanctuaries.

DON'T MISS

*** Lower Zambezi National Park: spectacular game-viewing from a wide choice of camps and lodges.
*** Canoeing on the Lower Zambezi: paddle along one of Africa's mightiest rivers.
** Kariba Dam: view the imposing concrete wall that is said to have angered the Zambezi river god, Nyaminyami.
** Lake Kariba: charter a house-boat for a few days' fishing or visit the wilderness sanctuaries of Cheté and Chikana islands.

Opposite: *Close encounter during a canoe safari on the Lower Zambezi.*

SAFETY ON SAFARI

On safari, you may be surprised at how indifferent some animals appear in the presence of people, but remember that they are still very much wild animals. Always keep a safe distance and never leave your vehicle or stray from your walking safari or canoeing guide. Few, if any, camps in Zambia have fences to keep animals out, so respect the fact that you are a privileged visitor in a wild environment and act accordingly.

LOWER ZAMBEZI NATIONAL PARK ★★★

After the chaotic turbulence of Victoria Falls and the confinement of Lake Kariba, the Zambezi River enters a gentle, unimpeded phase as it slowly spreads out across the Lower Zambezi valley. Over the millennia, the river has left traces of its wanderings in the form of abandoned watercourses and pools. These, along with silt-enriched islands and flood plains, have created a densely vegetated, wildlife-rich haven protected by the 4092km^2 (1579 sq mile) Lower Zambezi National Park.

Although animals (and tourists) are concentrated near the river, the park also encompasses the higher ground of the rift valley escarpment rising to the north. These slopes are covered in broadleaf woodland which gives way to mopane forest interspersed with winterthorn acacia on the valley floor. Closer to the river, the vegetation becomes more riotous with other species, like fig and ebony, jostling for space.

Across the Zambezi lies Zimbabwe's Mana Pools National Park. It is not unusual for elephants and other wildlife to swim from one country to the other – benefiting from the protected areas lining both sides of the river.

Wildlife

The Lower Zambezi National Park is one of the best places in Zambia to see **elephant**. Herds of more than 100 individuals are a spectacular sight. After one or two days in the park, you may well have identified a good repertoire of elephant behaviour – from sleeping under the shady canopy of the winterthorns to wading across river channels in search of fresh island forage.

Buffalo are another common sight. Herds of several hundred can often be seen grazing on islands, flocks of cattle egrets flapping around them like loose laundry. Other large mammals include hippo

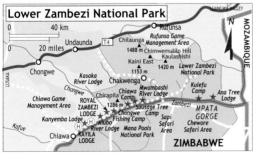

Lower Zambezi National Park

Left: *Stopping to enjoy a 'sundowner' drink at sunset is a long-standing safari tradition.*
Opposite: *Elephants use their versatile trunks to reach the seed pods of winterthorn acacias in the Lower Zambezi National Park.*

and zebra, plus a variety of antelopes such as waterbuck, kudu, impala, eland, bushbuck and wildebeest. Unfortunately, black rhino were eradicated by poachers in the 1980s and the national park is also conspicuous for its absence of giraffe.

Lower Zambezi National Park has a healthy population of **predators** – among them several thriving prides of lion. Leopard are also occasionally spotted during night drives, along with other nocturnal species such as honey badger, hyena, porcupine and civet. If you are very lucky you may spot a cheetah.

The **bird life** is stunning. The dramatic, almost gull-like, cry of the African fish eagle is quintessential Zambezi. Look out for these majestic raptors perched on dead trees near the water's edge or, if you are very lucky, swooping down to snatch a fish with outstretched talons. Other commonly sighted species include white-fronted bee-eaters which dig into the sandy river bank to create nesting colonies. Watch them darting from half-submerged branches to catch flying insects. Pied, giant and malachite kingfishers also haunt the river margins, along with cormorants, egrets and storks. For something a little more unusual, keep your binoculars handy for red-winged pratincole, narina trogon and Meyer's parrot.

ELEPHANT

Scientific name:
Loxodonta africana.
Vital statistics: length from tail to tip of outstretched trunk up to 7.5m (25ft); weight up to 6000kg (13,200lb).
Distinguishing features: huge ears and elongated nose and upper lip.
Habitat: swamps, forests, grasslands, arid areas.
Diet: up to 200kg (450lb) of vegetation daily.
Breeding: 22-month gestation period, 1 calf.
Likes: overripe fruit, other elephants.
Dislikes: lion, hyena, wild dog and crocodiles which can attack weak calves.

Right: *Weighing up to 700kg (1540lb), buffalo are frequently encountered in the Lower Zambezi National Park.*
Opposite: *Keen anglers should consider staying at Chongwe Fishing Camp which offers time-share chalets from May–Oct.*

HIPPOPOTAMUS

Scientific name:
Hippopotamus amphibius.
Vital statistics: length up to 4.2m (14ft); weight up to 3200kg (7050lb).
Distinguishing features: large, curved lower canines up to 45cm (18in) in length.
Habitat: water deep enough to submerge in, grassland within commuting distance.
Diet: grass which it plucks with muscular lips, mainly at night.
Breeding: eight-month gestation, usually one calf.
Likes: oxpecker birds and certain fish which pick parasites from their skin.
Dislikes: large crocodiles near their young.

How to Visit

The least complicated way to visit the Lower Zambezi is to book an all-inclusive safari with one of the lodges or camps in and around the national park. A typical package will include transfers (either driving overland or flying by light aircraft into Jeki Airstrip inside the park), accommodation, meals, as well as guided wildlife-viewing activities.

One highly rewarding alternative is to join a **multi-day canoe trip** (with fully supported camps en route) and paddle your way down the Zambezi. A third option is to **drive yourself**. Obviously, only the adventurous and experienced should consider independent travel. Two well-equipped 4x4 vehicles will be required to tackle the rough tracks of the escarpment that lead into Lower Zambezi National Park – one is a safety precaution in case the other breaks down.

ACTIVITIES
Game Drives and Walks ★★★

As well as traditional **game drives** (most rewarding during early morning and late afternoon when the midday heat has subsided and animals are more active), many camps and lodges can arrange **night drives** and **walking safaris**. Do not, however, be tempted to wander off on your own. With the Lower Zambezi's high densities of elephant, buffalo and hippo, this can be extremely dangerous. There is also little point in going off to explore when a couple of hours sitting quietly in your camp will often yield numerous sightings of birds and other wildlife.

Fishing ★★

Many lodges in the area provide rods and tackle. The Lower Zambezi, home to 75 fish species, offers one of the finest freshwater angling experiences in the world. As well as tiger fish and bream, one of the most sought-after species is vundu – a type of large catfish which is apparently lured by strong-smelling soap.

Canoe Trips ★★★

Everything from a one-hour paddle in a quiet backwater to a ten-day camping expedition is available. Canoeing on the Zambezi might appear to be an epic undertaking. However, as long as you go with the flow and remember to knock before entering hippo territory, it is actually a very relaxing and rewarding way to spot the Lower Zambezi's wildlife.

It is true that surprised hippos can be irritable and, with their impressive tusk-like canines, they do appear to be well equipped to dice you into Zambezi-style ratatouille. Just remember that regular tapping on the side of your canoe usually makes them surface and allows you to steer clear. Your guide will also be well aware of the locations of the various hippo pods, allowing you to observe the extraordinary, bubbling, grunting antics of these wonderful creatures from a respectful distance. As for crocodiles – don't worry. No sooner will you have spotted one basking on a sandbank than the chances

> **MULTI-DAY TRIPS**
>
> The **Great Zambezi Trail** is a four-day canoeing safari operated by Safari Par Excellence (*see* page 61) from May–Oct. It covers about 60km (37 miles) of the Zambezi between the Kafue River confluence and the Chakwenga River, with overnight stops at various lodges. No previous canoeing experience is necessary – simple techniques of steering and stability will be taught on day one. Although the pace is gentle, there are occasional headwinds that can make paddling quite tiring. These are often strongest during August.

LOCAL CURIOS

In the Lake Kariba area look out for Nyaminyami sticks – wooden carvings depicting the serpent-headed Zambezi river god. Curios are also available at some of the lodges in the Lower Zambezi National Park area, but you will pay premium prices compared to markets in Lusaka and Livingstone.

Below: *Canadian-style canoes are stable and simple to manoeuvre in the calm channels of the Zambezi River.*

are it will slip quietly into the water and vanish from view. Nothing in the Zambezi is intent on tipping you out of your canoe.

A **typical canoe trip** from a camp or lodge in or near the park will involve two or three hours of intermittent paddling and drifting. Two-person, Canadian-style canoes are usually used. They have plenty of leg room and, more importantly if it's a sundowner trip, there's also space for a cool box packed with drinks.

The huge advantage of canoeing over other forms of safari transport is the absence of a noisy engine. Imagine drifting silently past a group of browsing elephants and being able to hear their stomachs rumbling! Under paddle-power, keen bird-watchers may well be able to pinpoint rarities by their calls, while photographers will have none of the potential vibration problems of taking pictures from a vehicle.

Generally speaking, distance is not a great issue when it comes to canoeing on the Zambezi. You will probably see (and hear) more by slowly exploring a few hundred metres than by charging off into the distance in a blur of blazing paddles. However, if you have the time to spare there are several superb options for **overnight canoe safaris**, lasting anything from three to ten days.

The Lower Zambezi can be canoed from Kariba Dam to its confluence with the Luangwa River at the Mozambique border – a distance of around 200km (125 miles). Most people choose to canoe a shorter, three- or four-day section – the most popular lying between Chirundu and the Lower Zambezi National Park. Two other interesting sections include Kariba Gorge and, slightly further downstream, Mpata Gorge.

Lake Kariba ★★

It was an audacious feat of engineering. Over a period of five years, from 1955–1960, hundreds of workers succeeded in damming the Zambezi River. The end result, Lake Kariba, flooded 290km (180 miles) of the Lower Zambezi valley to a width of 32km (20 miles). At the time of its completion, Kariba Dam was the world's largest – 128m (420ft) high and up to 26m (85ft) thick – an emphatic concrete plug that had swallowed something like a million cubic metres of cement!

The dam's two power stations now have a combined generating capacity of 1320MW, supplying Zambia's Copperbelt and various parts of Zimbabwe with a crucial source of electricity. However, much was sacrificed in the pursuit of power. Over 80 workers were killed during the dam's construction (18 of whom lie entombed in the dam itself), while 57,000 Batonga villagers were resettled as their homelands became inundated.

In 1959, Operation Noah rescued some 6000 animals, including 40 black rhinoceros, threatened with drowning as the lake filled. Many more perished. Among them, strange as it seems, were fish like the eel which found its migration route to the sea suddenly blocked. But other wildlife, such as crocodile, hippopotamus and buffalo

Above: *Skeletons of drowned trees bear testimony to the artificial creation of Lake Kariba.*

DAM STATISTICS

At the time of its completion in 1959, Lake Kariba was the world's largest man-made lake. At maximum capacity, the lake has a surface area of 5200km² (2000 sq miles) and a depth of 116m (380ft). It is 290km (180 miles) in length and reaches a width of 32km (20 miles). The dam wall, which reaches a height of 128m (420ft) along its 617m (2025ft) length, required over 1,000,000m³ of concrete.

flourished in the swelling waters of Lake Kariba. Another fish, the sardine-like kapenta, was introduced to Kariba from Lake Tanganyika in 1967 and now forms the basis of a thriving fishing industry.

Kariba Dam **

Located at the eastern end of the lake, Kariba Dam can be visited from nearby Siavonga (see below). A walk along the top of the dam wall provides stomach-lurching views into a gorge on the one side and more tranquil vistas of the lake on the other. An interesting display describes the dam's construction and some of the hefty statistics involved.

Siavonga *

Compared to the Zimbabwean shore of Lake Kariba, the Zambian side is relatively undeveloped for tourism. The small town of Siavonga has the most facilities – although much of these are geared towards conference trade from Lusaka.

As well as a base from which to visit Kariba Dam, Siavonga offers water sports, such as windsurfing, water-skiing and paragliding. Some lodges also organize sundowner cruises to enjoy Kariba's acclaimed sunsets. A more unusual evening boat trip visits one of the lake's kapenta fishing rigs from which local people use spotlights to lure the protein-rich fish into their nets.

Below: *Kariba Dam tames the Zambezi and generates electricity for both Zambia and Zimbabwe.*

Most sport anglers visit Lake Kariba for the thrill of catching tiger fish, a tenacious beast renowned for its speed and strength.

A peaceful way of experiencing the lake (and perhaps doing a spot of fishing at the same time) is to hire a houseboat. Other attractions in the area include

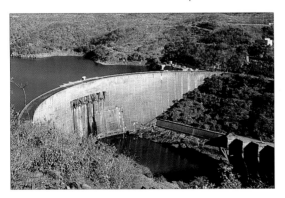

a crocodile farm west of Siavonga, and the Chirundu Fossil Forest which contains the petrified remains of trees believed to be over 150 million years old.

Above: *Fishing for sardine-like kapenta is an important industry for local people at Lake Kariba.*

Sinazongwe ★

Located near the western end of Lake Kariba, the kapenta fishing village of Sinazongwe has fewer tourist facilities than Siavonga. Each May it hosts a tiger fishing competition and it is also the transfer point to both Cheté and Chikana islands.

Westlake Islands ★

With an area of 27km² (10 sq miles), **Cheté Island** is the largest in Lake Kariba. A private wildlife reserve and bird sanctuary, it lies 27km (17 miles) from Sinazongwe in a remote corner of the lake tucked up against the Zimbabwean shore. Cheté has a lodge (facing west for those memorable sunsets) which organizes walking, boating and canoeing safaris in search of elephant, waterbuck, kudu, lion and leopard. A 10m (33ft) trimaran is also available for sailing and fishing cruises.

At just 2.5km² (1 sq mile), nearby **Chikana Island** (actually three seperate islands) is much smaller than Cheté. However, it also provides impressive wildlife-viewing and fishing. Both islands are remote. Just reaching them by boat can be an adventure in itself – and once there, they offer a true touch of the Zambian wilderness.

KAPENTA

A small sardine-like fish once indigenous to Lake Tanganyika, kapenta was introduced to Lake Kariba where it now thrives. Local fishermen catch kapenta at night using spotlights to lure the fish into their nets. It is then dried, fried or made into a relish. Baskets of dried kapenta are sold throughout Zambia.

The Lower Zambezi and Lake Kariba at a Glance

Although many lodges and canoeing operators are open from **Apr–Nov**, the best time to visit is **Jun–Sep**. Game-viewing by boat is possible year-round, although from late October, temperatures can become unbearably hot – occasionally soaring to 45°C (113°F). Angling is best from **Sep–Oct** when tiger fish are more active. Bird-watching, although excellent year-round, is particularly rewarding from **Dec–Apr**.

Lower Zambezi National Park
The quickest and most direct way to the park is by a 40-minute **light aircraft** from Lusaka, followed by a **4x4 transfer** to your lodge. **Overland transfers** from Lusaka to various camps and lodges in and around the park are also available – some may involve a short boat trip. It is also possible to join a **canoe safari** from Chirundu, paddle downstream and then fly or drive out. **Independent travel** by 4x4 should only be considered by the experienced and well prepared.

Lake Kariba
Siavonga, on the lake's north-eastern shore, is a two-and-a-half-hour car drive (longer by bus) from Lusaka on well-surfaced roads. Most of the four-hour route from Lusaka to Sinazongwe is on tarmac or all-weather gravel roads. Cheté

and Chikana islands can be reached by chartered light aircraft from Livingstone and boat transfers from Sinazongwe.

Lower Zambezi National Park
All camps and lodges operate game drives and many also have walking or canoe trips. Accompanied by guides, these provide the best means of encountering wildlife.

Lake Kariba
Some lodges in Siavonga arrange tours in the area, as well as stays on houseboats. For maximum flexibility, however, you will need your own transport.

Lower Zambezi National Park
There are numerous lodges and camps in the park and surrounding game management areas. Most are close to the river and all offer excellent wildlife-viewing opportunities as well as activities, such as canoeing, game drives, walks and fishing. Staying at the up-market lodges or camps usually involves booking a safari package which includes transfers, accommodation, meals and activities. Independent travellers will be able to find one or two self-catering options.

LUXURY LODGES AND TENTED CAMPS
Ana Tree Lodge, PO Box

32661, Lusaka, tel: (01) 287 508, fax: 250 730, email: anatreelodge@zamnet.zm, www.anatreelodge.com Opened 2004, eight twin-bedded luxury *en-suite* tents.
Chiawa Camp, PO Box 30972, Lusaka, tel: (01) 261 588, fax: 262 683, e-mail: info@chiawa.zm website: www.chiawa.com Small, family-run seasonal camp within national park, *en-suite* tents for 16 guests, full range of activities, eight-bed Old Mondoro Bush Camp.
Chongwe River Camp, PO Box CA 102, Castle Post Office, Lusaka. Tel/fax: (01) 261 286 808, email: info@chongwe.com, website: www.chongwe-river.com Located at the confluence of the Chongwe and Zambezi rivers, shaded setting under magnificent winter thorn acacias, six tented chalets under thatch, each with luxury open-air *en-suite* bathroom; specialises in walking safaris, but game drives, canoeing and fishing also available.
Kanyemba Lodge, PO Box 38837, Lusaka, tel: (97) 755 720, email: info@kanyemba.com, website: www.kanyemba.com Opened 2002, five chalets, honeymoon suite, private verandahs overlooking Zambezi.
Kasaka River Lodge, PO Box 320197, Lusaka, tel: (01) 265 836, fax: 260 012, email: bookings@kasakariverlodge.

The Lower Zambezi and Lake Kariba at a Glance

com, website: www.kasaka riverlodge.com Opened 2001, eight chalets, honeymoon suite, pool.

Kayila Lodge, Safari Par Excellence, *see* page 61 for details. Small, exclusive lodge in a private wildlife sanctuary.

Kiambi Lower Zambezi, PO Box 35196, Northway, 4065 Durban, South Africa; tel: (27 31) 563 9774, fax: 563 1957, email: info@kiambi.co.za, website: www.kiambi.co.za Eight tented chalets on raised wooden platforms, some with views of Kanyemba Island; dining and bar area, pool, activities ranging from boat cruises and game drives to fishing and bush walks.

Kulefu Camp, Star of Africa, see page 41. Eight spacious tents on raised platforms at river's edge, remote location, prolific wildlife.

Redcliff Zambezi Lodge, PO Box 12609, Clubview, 0014, South Africa, tel: (27 12) 653 2664, fax: 654 4015, e-mail: info@redcliff-lodge.com website: www.redcliff-lodge.com Four twin tented chalets and two family chalets overlook river beyond eastern edge of national park, fly fishing, birdwatching and game drives.

Royal Zambezi Lodge, Lion Roars Safaris, PO Box 638, Greenacres, Port Elizabeth, 6057, South Africa, tel: (27 41) 374 0553, email: lionroars@mweb.co.za website: www.royalzambezi.com Thatch-sheltered tents accommodating up to 24 guests,

beautiful riverside setting outside park, spectacular bar overlooking river.

Sausage Tree Camp, PO Box 35139, Lusaka, tel: (01) 212 597, fax: 272 456, email: info@sausagetreecamp.com website: sausagetreecamp.com Six capacious, chic Bedouin-style *en-suite* tents, position in heart of national park overlooking channels teeming with wildlife, canoeing.

MID-RANGE/BUDGET
SELF-CATERING CAMPS
Mvuu Lodge, PO Box 1139, Vanderbjilpark, 1900, South Africa, tel: (27 16) 987 1837, fax: 16 987 2655, e-mail: info@mvuulodge.com website: www.mvuulodge.com Fully inclusive or self-catering tented camp, plus camp site; game drives, canoeing, fishing.

Lake Kariba
LUXURY
Cheté Island Safari Lodge, PO Box 88, Sinazongwe, tel: (260 99) 415 594, e-mail: reservations@cheteisland.com website: www.cheteisland.com *En-suite* tents, sailing cruises, walking safaris, canoeing, fishing, swimming pool.

LUXURY/MID-RANGE
Chikana Island, Gwembe Safaris, PO Box 630162, Choma, tel: (03) 220 169, fax: 220 054, e-mail: info@gwembesafaris.com, website: www.gwembe safaris.com As well as a 10-

bed camp on Chikana Island, Gwembe operate Lake View (Lake Kariba) and Gwembe Safari Lodge (Choma).

MID-RANGE
Lake Kariba Inn, PO Box 177, Siavonga, tel: (01) 511 358, fax: 511 249. 35 rooms, lake cruises, fishing trips, can arrange four-day cruises on Matusadona houseboat.

Lake Safari Lodge, PO Box 30, Siavonga, tel: (01) 511 148, fax: 511 103. Comfortable hotel, good pool and watersports.

BUDGET
Eagle's Rest Chalets, PO Box 1, Siavonga, tel/fax: (01) 511 168. 18 self-catering chalets, nearby camp ground, canoeing trips, houseboat cruises.

SHOPPING

In the Lake Kariba area look out for Nyaminyami sticks – wooden carvings depicting the serpent-headed Zambezi river god. Curios are also available at some lodges in the Lower Zambezi National Park area, but you will pay premium prices compared to markets in Lusaka and Livingstone.

TOURS AND EXCURSIONS

Multi-day Canoeing Trips
The **Great Zambezi Trail** is a four-day canoeing safari operated from May–Oct by Safari Par Excellence (*see* page 61). It covers about 60km (37 miles) of the Zambezi.

5
The Luangwa Valley

Pulsing through a broad rift valley on its journey south towards the Zambezi, the Luangwa River threads a vibrant lifeline between four of Zambia's wildest and most remote national parks. The undisputed jewel in this chain is **South Luangwa National Park**. Long renowned as *the* place in Africa for **walking safaris**, its lavish spread of dappled woodlands, lazy river channels and lily-covered lagoons has abundant wildlife and is perfect for exploring on foot.

On a walking safari your senses are fine-tuned to every crackle of leaf, whiff of dung or the slightest movement. Anticipation floods your body with adrenaline and you feel a primitive, instinctive bond with your surroundings. But what truly sets South Luangwa apart from walking safaris in other parts of Africa is the expertise of the guides. Every few minutes they will pause to reveal a nugget of bush-lore or identify one of South Luangwa's 400-odd bird species.

There are several, mainly up-market, camps and lodges in South Luangwa National Park – all offering traditional **game drives** (by day and night) in addition to walking safaris. Your chances of spotting leopard are excellent. There are also over 15,000 elephant and a similar number of hippo. Unique to the region are Thornicroft's giraffe and Cookson's wildebeest.

North Luangwa National Park has fewer facilities and mainly caters for off-the-beaten-track walking safaris. **Luambe National Park** and **Lukusuzi National Park** are even more remote – requiring plenty of time and experience for a well-planned expedition.

DON'T MISS

*** South Luangwa National Park: a beautiful reserve with Africa's finest game-viewing.
*** Walking safari: originally developed in the Luangwa Valley and still a superb way of experiencing the area.
*** Night drive: probably your best chance of spotting leopard in Zambia.
*** Kawaza Village: an opportunity to immerse yourself in Zambian village life.
** North Luangwa National Park: highly rewarding walking in remote and little-visited wilderness.

Opposite: *Impala – always alert for any signs of danger.*

South Luangwa
National Park

SOUTH LUANGWA NATIONAL PARK ★★★

Bordered by the Muchinga Escarpment to the west and the Luangwa River to the east, South Luangwa National Park covers an area of 9050km² (3493 sq miles). It comprises a rich mosaic of habitats – from dense mopane forest and riverside woodland to open grassland plains and sheltered pools.

Thriving on the mineral-rich soils deposited by the Luangwa River and its tributaries, the park contains some fine mahogany, ebony, marula and tamarind trees. Also widespread is the sausage tree – so called for the enormous pendulous fruits that hang from its branches.

It is the sheer density of wildlife, however, that elevates South Luangwa into the ranks of Africa's great game areas such as the Serengeti, Okavango, Etosha and Kruger. Once known as 'The Crowded Place', its elephant population used to exceed 100,000 before the poaching scourge of the 1980s. Nevertheless, over 15,000 of these magnificent creatures still roam the park, along with most of the large mammals you would expect to find in a thriving African reserve. In fact, only the rhinoceros, which sadly succumbed to the poachers, will elude visitors.

Below: *The Luangwa Valley has one of Africa's highest concentrations of hippopotamus.*

History

Many years before South Luangwa was declared a national park in February 1972, the region was well known to European ex-plorers, hunters, traders and missionaries. In 1866, Livingstone crossed the Luangwa River just to the south of the present-day Chibembe camp.

However, it was during the mid-1900s that another visionary man, Norman Carr, came to influence the development of South Luangwa National Park. Originally appointed as a game ranger for a fledgling trio of game reserves established during 1938, Carr worked with the local Senior Chief Nsefu to extend reserve boundaries and to ensure that villagers received income from the region's first safari camps. In addition to tirelessly promoting conservation issues, he went on to pioneer the concept of walking safaris and, in 1986, he built Kapani Lodge. It was his home until his death a decade later.

Above: *Most camps and lodges in South Luangwa National Park provide quality accommodation, elaborate meals and expert guiding – despite being located somewhere that is remote and often inaccessible during the wet season.*

Wildlife

Benefiting from a huge area, diverse habitats and deep-rooted conservation, South Luangwa National Park supports abundant and varied wildlife. At one end of the scale are large herds of elephant and buffalo, hippos that virtually clog the rivers, and prolific big cats. At the other end of the scale are dung beetles, termites, antlions, frogs and a myriad other mini-beasts. In South Luangwa, cour-tesy of its well-practised combination of vehicle and walking safaris, you will encounter both extremes – the typical safari 'megafauna' as well as the subtle details at your feet.

Since much of the accommodation in the park is located near a river, the first animal you are likely to become familiar with is the **hippopotamus**. Emerging at

WALKING SAFARI CODE

- Walk slowly and quietly.
- Pause often to savour the sights, smells and sounds of the African bush.
- Never stray from your guide or armed scout.
- Never run in the rare event of being charged, but stay calm and follow your guide's instructions.
- Drink plenty of water and cover up in the sun.
- Keep a pair of binoculars handy on a waist belt.
- Wear lightweight boots with thorn-resistant soles and ankle support.

Above: *South Luangwa may well be your best chance in Zambia to spot a leopard.*
Opposite: *Thornicroft's giraffe is only found in the Luangwa Valley.*

ANCIENT VALLEY

The Luangwa Valley, like the Great Rift Valley to the north, was created by faulting in the earth's crust. This began up to 300 million years ago and also led to the formation of the Lower Zambezi Valley. In more recent times, the Luangwa River and its tributaries have been constantly reshaping the valley floor, creating new watercourses and abandoning old ones as isolated oxbow lakes and wide grassy corridors.

dusk to graze on land, hippos spend much of the day lounging about in rivers with just their eyes, nostrils and ears visible. While submerged, shoals of personal aquatic hygienists (in the form of hungry fish) pick off parasites and dead skin from the hippos' hides. Above water, oxpecker birds perform a similar service to ears and nostrils – presumably a ticklish experience judging by the extraordinary grunting outbursts of 'laughter' frequently heard in the vicinity of a hippo pod! The best time to observe hippopotamus is during the dry season when shrinking watercourses concentrate them into dense congregations.

Other common animals found in South Luangwa are the **antelopes**. Fourteen species occur here, the most widespread being puku and impala. Search for kudu and bushbuck in more densely vegetated areas and waterbuck (both defassa and common varieties) near lagoons and rivers. Sable and roan antelopes are mainly encountered in the hilly region bordering the escarpment, while eland tend to favour the Nsefu Sector of the park. Common duiker, reedbuck, grysbok and oribi are also present, but their shy and retiring nature makes them difficult to spot.

Part of the thinking behind declaring South Luangwa a national park was to protect its two **endemic species** – animals only found within the valley. Thornicroft's giraffe, a rare subspecies, is distinguished from the more widespread southern giraffe by its darker body patches. Cookson's wildebeest, South Luangwa's other 'speciality', is a subspecies of the blue wildebeest and possesses a greyish-red coat.

With no shortage of potential prey, large **predators** such as lions, leopards and hyenas do well in the Luangwa Valley. In fact, South Luangwa National Park's leopard population is thought to be one of the densest on the continent, with one animal per 2.5km² (1 sq mile). Game drives by night are deservedly popular in the park, providing thrilling spotlit opportunities for watching these impressive nocturnal felines stalking puku fawns – one of their favourite food items.

Among the host of other creatures active at night are some wonderful **birds**, including the giant eagle owl and pennant-winged nightjar. During the day, other avian highlights include several varieties of water bird. Yellow-billed storks wade the shallows, kicking up the mud with their feet to reveal hidden morsels of food. Another long-legged species, the crowned crane, gathers in large flocks on the salt pans.

LUANGWA'S ENDEMICS

The **South Luangwa National Park** was declared on 15 February 1972. As well as protecting a wide range of wildlife-rich habitats, including rivers, woodland, and grassland, the park safeguards the endemic Thornicroft's giraffe and Cookson's wildebeest.

During September and October, watch out for the lavishly coloured carmine bee-eater which nests in river banks. Around this time, you can't miss the vast, pulsing clouds of red-billed quelea streaming back and forth to drink at the river's edge. Remember to look twice at a tree covered with exceptionally green leaves – they could be Lillian's lovebirds!

Below: *When startled, the warthog can reach an impressive pace, well-deserving of its nickname, 'The Kalahari Ferrari'.*

How to Visit

The majority of visitors to South Luangwa National Park prearrange safari packages which include flights to nearby Mfuwe airport, transfers into the national park, accommodation, meals and guided game-viewing activities. Even if you decide to travel by one of the three overland routes (from Chipata, Mpika or Petauke), the chances are that you will pass through the Mfuwe area.

Mfuwe

Located a short distance east of the national park, **Mfuwe International Airport** is the rather grandiose title for what amounts to a small terminal building and a scattering of light aircraft used by local pilots to probe even more far-flung airstrips inside the park and beyond. Nevertheless, with regular flights to and from Lusaka, this is where most South Luangwa safaris begin and end.

If you find yourself waiting for a flight or transfer into the park, relax with a drink at the nearby **Moondog Café** or browse the locally produced handicrafts at **Magenge Crafts**.

ACTIVITIES

Feet versus wheels. This is the dilemma facing many visitors with limited time in the South Luangwa National Park. On a typical game drive, using an open 4x4 vehicle, you can usually approach wildlife more closely than on a walking safari. Animals are far more skittish in the presence of people on foot. In a vehicle, your chances of spotting a wider range of species are also higher. Walking, however, provides a more intimate brush with nature. You will learn a great deal about animal tracks, plants, bush medicine and bird life. For many, simply the thrill of walking in one of Africa's last great wilderness areas is reward enough. The bottom line, perhaps, is to ensure that your safari has a good mixture of both foot and vehicle excursions – plus a few night drives and a visit to a local village.

Above: *Visitors enjoy a tea break during a morning game drive in South Luangwa National Park.*

Game Drives ★★★

Typically, camps will organize a couple of game drives each day – one in the early morning and another later in the afternoon. The second drive often incorporates a drink stop to watch the sunset before continuing on through the dusk using a spotlight to search for nocturnal animals.

Walking Safaris ★★★

Just as Lower Zambezi National Park is renowned for its canoeing, no visit to South Luangwa would be complete

---

LEOPARD

Scientific name:
Panthera pardus.
Vital statistics: length, including tail, up to 2.9m (10ft), weight up to 85kg (187lb).
Distinguishing features: spotted coat, short limbs, long tail.
Habitat: widespread.
Diet: anything up to small–medium antelopes.
Breeding: up to 110-day gestation, 1–4 cubs.
Likes: caching its kill in trees away from lions and hyenas.
Dislikes: other adult leopards intruding on its territory.

without at least sampling a walking safari. There are three ways of doing this. If a sample is, indeed, all you are after, then most if not all of the camps and lodges can arrange short **walking excursions**. A few, such as Star of Africa Kapani, have gone a step further by creating **multiple-day walking trails**, sleeping overnight in rustic, but fully serviced bush camps. A third alternative is the so-called **mobile safari** operated by Robin Pope Safaris, in which all camping gear is transferred by a support vehicle to each night's stop.

Safety

One of the first things people want to know before embarking on a walking safari is, 'Are there any lions around?' The answer is invariably 'yes – plenty of them.' But before you tear off your walking shoes and sprint for the nearest Land Rover, remember that wild animals are usually extremely wary of humans on foot. All walking safaris are led by an armed scout. Before setting off you will be briefed on safety – never wander off on your own or walk in front of your scout and, in the unlikely event of being charged, don't run but follow your guide's instructions.

Stepping Out

A walking safari provides a complete workout for the senses. Threading single-file through the bush – like hominids from a distant past – you will have the opportunity to discover the sights, sounds, smells and even tastes of the African wilderness.

Each dawn, faithfully printed on game trails and sandy clearings, there is a fresh edition of the so-called 'Bushman's newspaper' – the tracks and signs left by animals the previous night. Your guide will be able to interpret everything, from the subtly wrinkled oval craters stamped in the ground by a bull elephant to the gashes and scuffs from a zebra's flaying hooves as it took a dust bath.

Be prepared for the fact that your guide will be fascinated by animal droppings! No offering will be passed by without a detailed inspection. Dung can reveal a great deal about the wildlife in the area, including what species it came from and how recently. Clues to diet can also be teased out. A leopard scat may contain the undigested remains of fur, while hyena droppings are often dry and chalky – a result of the scavenger's habit of crunching up bones.

A walking safari is not a mad chase to tick off the big five. It's all about walking slowly, pausing often to marvel at small wonders – the egg cocoon of a praying mantis which the female fashions from her spit; a shed cobra skin turned inside out; the wandering tunnels of sand that termites build to protect themselves from predators and sunburn.

Opposite: *Following an armed scout in single file enables you to appreciate subtle natural details.*
Below: *Fresh lion tracks draw attention and set the spine tingling.*

VILLAGE ETIQUETTE

When visiting a local village try to minimize the potential negative impacts that western culture could have on traditional lifestyles by observing the following code:

• Dress modestly. Women should wear a *chitenge* (wrap-around skirt), long dress or trousers.

• Always ask permission before taking photographs or video footage.

• Refrain from over-the-top public displays of affection. It is not a local custom and villagers may find it embarrassing.

• Resist giving money or gifts directly to villagers as this may demean local people by encouraging begging. By all means make donations to local community projects, such as schools, etc.

• Learn a little of the local language (such as a greeting) and bring photographs from home to help you share aspects of your own culture.

Many of the plants you will encounter are deep-rooted in ancient bush medicine. A salve from the sausage tree treats eczema; bush lavender tea clears nasal congestion, while the tart fruit of the tamarind tree is a powerful laxative.

Don't become frustrated if the only wildlife you spot during an hour's walk is the retreating posterior of a startled warthog. During your walking safari you may, of course, be extremely lucky and get a close-up view of elephants from the cover of a termite mound – but treat this as a bonus.

River Safaris ★

Walking safaris are strictly a dry season proposition. Apart from a few lodges in the Mfuwe area, most accommodation is seasonal. However, between February and April, **river safaris** operate in the park using Tafika Camp as a base for canoeing forays. With the Luangwa River in full flood, flowing at up to 8km/h (5mph) and 5m (16ft) higher than October dry season levels, these exciting trips offer a completely different perspective of the national park. They are particularly recommended for bird watchers who will be riveted by the large nesting colonies of herons and yellow-billed storks. As an intrepid additional option, a **microlight** is sometimes available for breathtaking aerial 'green season' views of the Luangwa Valley.

Right: *Local children spontaneously pose for a photograph in a village near South Luangwa National Park.*

Cultural Visits ★★

The Luangwa Valley is home to around 35,000 Kunda people – traditionally hunters, but now mainly living as subsistence farmers cultivating crops like maize, sorghum, soya bean and mango. Aware of the economic and community benefits that wildlife tourism could bring, two villages have launched cultural tourism enterprises, offering visitors an authentic insight into their traditional culture and lifestyles.

Above: *Remote national parks with little or no tourist infrastructure, like Luambe and Lukusuzi, require self-sufficient 4x4 expeditions.*

Nsendamila Cultural Village is located in the Mfuwe area, close to the entrance gate to the national park. Named after the huge baobab tree which stands in the middle of a collection of mud and thatch rondavels, Nsendamila demonstrates several aspects of Kunda life. A blacksmith produces axes, hoes and other tools using a hammer and anvil, women pound maize, while traditional dances are held beneath the baobab. Visitors will also get a chance to sample staple *nsima* porridge, and purchase locally made carvings and woven mats.

Kawaza Village Tourism Project invites tourists to stay overnight in the village, sleeping in traditional huts and participating in Kunda daily life. Not only is this an excellent way of meeting local people and seeing how they live, but there is minimal impact from tourism on the community. Local villagers will show you around the area, including a visit to a school, a church and even a traditional healer. You will be able to discuss conservation and development issues with the senior chief and take part in everyday life – fetching water, collecting firewood, working in the fields, brewing beer, traditional dancing, storytelling, pounding maize and cooking over an open fire.

SPOTTED HYENA

Scientific name:
Crocuta crocuta.
Vital statistics: length up to 1.7m (6ft), weight up to 80kg (176lb).
Distinguishing features: heavy muzzle, sloping hindquarters.
Habitat: savannas, woodlands, arid areas.
Diet: carrion and live prey, hunted down in packs.
Breeding: 4-month gestation, 1–2 cubs.
Likes: ganging up on lions and cheetahs and driving them off their kills.
Dislikes: persistent vultures at a kill.

Apart from the shared experiences of cultural visits, the income they generate is crucial to local employment and improving school and health facilities. Farming in the Luangwa Valley is tough – animals raid crops and the seasons are harsh. A cultural visit will not only make a fascinating addition to your safari, it will also help to forge the ever-important link between the communities living outside the park and the wildlife protected within.

NORTH LUANGWA NATIONAL PARK ★★

With an area of 4636km² (1789 sq miles) North Luangwa National Park is half the size of its southern partner. Sandwiched between the Luangwa River and Muchinga Escarpment, it shares many of the plants and animals you would expect to find in South Luangwa. But there the similarities end. North Luangwa National Park is almost pure wilderness. There are no permanent lodges. Only a few safari operators are granted concessions in the area, using small bush camps from which to operate walking safaris and limited game drives.

GOING IT ALONE

Planning an independent safari can be a bewildering process. But if you find yourself wallowing in logistics like a proverbial hippo, spare a thought for whoever organized Lord Randolph Churchill's safari in 1892. In addition to seven wagons and a staff of over 30, Churchill advanced into the African bush laden with 20 tonnes of supplies, including two dozen rifles, a piano and a generous quantity of eau de cologne. Small wonder that he never made his mark as a great hunter.

Poaching was rife in North Luangwa during the early 1980s, but it has now been largely quashed – thanks, in part, to American scientists Mark and Delia Owens who described their anti-poaching efforts in the best-seller, *Survivor's Song*.

The park now supports large herds of buffalo and a good population of lion. Elephant and leopard can also be seen, along with Cookson's wildebeest, eland, hartebeest and reedbuck. A black rhino reintroduction scheme was successfully initiated in 2003.

LUAMBE AND LUKUSUZI NATIONAL PARKS ★

Located to the east of South Luangwa National Park, Luambe and Lukusuzi are remote, largely trackless parks covered in mopane and miombo woodland. Luambe National Park covers an area of 254km² (98 sq miles) and is thought to be a stronghold for Cookson's wildebeest, while the 2720km² (1050 sq miles) Lukusuzi National Park has granite outcrops favoured by the klipspringer. However, since reaching either park requires a self-sufficient 4x4 expedition, they are rarely visited.

Opposite and below:
The hunter and the hunted. Lions often trail herds of buffalo (their favourite quarry), but it requires teamwork and stealth to bring down such heavy and well-defended prey.

The Luangwa Valley at a Glance

Walking safaris in South Luangwa National Park are usually only possible from **Jun–Oct**. The park becomes flooded during summer – opening up the possibility of river trips, but closing down many camps which have to be reconstructed each May or June when flood waters recede. Some lodges are open longer, depending on access. Warm, sunny days and chilly nights typify the dry winter months from **Jun–Aug**. By **Oct–Nov**, however, temperatures can reach 45°C (113°F). Wildlife concentrates around shrinking lagoons towards the end of the dry season.

Scheduled daily **flights** from Lusaka provide the easiest and quickest way to reach South Luangwa National Park, taking about 1hr to reach the airport at Mfuwe. You can fly to Mfuwe from Lilongwe in Malawi. **Road transfers** by 4x4 from Mfuwe to and from your lodge or camp will be included as part of your safari package. If **driving yourself** to South Luangwa the best road is via Chipata. Other more adventurous routes lead from Petauke and Mpika – but need a **4x4**, preferably two, and lots of experience. To visit North Luangwa or any of the other remote areas, book an **organized trip** through a licensed operator.

Camps and lodges will take care of all internal travel arrangements, including airport transfers, game drives, walking safaris and boat trips.

South Luangwa National Park
LUXURY LODGES AND TENTED CAMPS

Most of the following are open from around May–Nov unless otherwise stated.

Bilimungwe, **Chamilandu**, **Chindeni**, **Kapamba and Kuyenda Bush Camps**, The Bushcamp Company, PO Box 91, Mfuwe, tel: (062) 45041, e-mail: alison@bushcampcompany.com website: www.bushcampcompany.com Rustic but high-quality camps linked by walking safari. Camps range from thatch chalets to tree houses with four-poster beds. The newest is Kapamba with four superb open-fronted chalets.

Chichele Presidential Lodge and Puku Ridge, Star of Africa, *see page 41*. Chichele: stunning lodge, ten air-conditioned rooms, with private terraces. Puku Ridge: tented camp for 12 guests.

Kafunta River Lodge and Island Bush Camp, PO Box 83, Mfuwe, tel: (062) 46046, email: kafunta@luangwa.com website: www.luangwa.com Impressive thatched lodge, eight wood and thatch

en-suite chalets, swimming pool. Open all year. Island Bush Camp is small and personal, located 2 hours south of the lodge.

Kaingo Camp and Mwamba Bushcamp, Shenton Safaris, PO Box 57, Mfuwe, tel: (062) 45064, email: info@kaingo.com website: www.kaingo.com Family-owned 12-bed lodge, wooden deck over river, six-bed bushcamp a three hour walk away.

Kapani River Lodge, Kakuli, Luwi, Mchenja and Nsolo Bushcamps, Norman Carr Safaris, PO Box 100, Mfuwe, tel: (062) 46015, fax: 45025, e-mail: kapani@normancarrsafaris.com website: www.normancarrsafaris.com Long-established thatched lodge overlooks lagoon, comfortable *en-suite* rooms for 20 guests, experienced guides, satellite bushcamps linked by walking safari. Lodge open all year. Mchenja Bushcamp opens in green season.

Lion Camp, tel: (2721) 421 3226, fax: 421 3227, email: lioncamp@iwayafrica.com, website: www.lioncamp.com Ten luxurious canvas and thatch chalets with air-con and *en-suite* bathrooms.

Mfuwe Lodge, PO Box 91, Mfuwe, tel: (062) 45041, fax: 45008, e-mail: alison@bushcampcompany.com website: www.mfuwelodge.com Large, stylish open-plan lodge located between two lagoons,

The Luangwa Valley at a Glance

18 beautifully furnished chalets, swimming pool. Open all year.

Tafika Camp and Chikoko Bushcamp, Remote Africa Safaris, PO Box 5, Mfuwe, e-mail: tafika@remoteafrica.com website: www.remoteafrica.com Superbly positioned reed and thatch chalets for 12 guests, microlight flights, river safaris Feb–Mar, walking safaris at Chikoko.

Tena Tena, Nkwali and Nsefu Camp, Robin Pope Safaris, PO Box 80, Mfuwe, tel: (062) 46090, fax: 46094, e-mail: info@robinpopesafaris.net website: www.robinpopesafaris.net Tena Tena: intimate and beautifully furnished camp for eight–ten guests, excellent guides; Nkwali: thatch and bamboo camp for 12 guests over looking Luangwa River; Nsefu: thatched rondavels in elegant 1950s style for 12 guests. Robin Pope Safaris also offer Luangwa Safari House, a stunning private house for eight guests, ideal for families.

BUDGET/MID-RANGE CAMPS
Flatdogs Camp,
Chibuli Guides and Tours, PO Box 125, Mfuwe, tel: (062) 46038, e-mail: info@flatdogscamp.com website: www.flatdogscamp.com Superb Jackal-Berry Tree House for up to four guests; six chalets; three-bedroom family house with kitchen; four classic safari tents; two campsites, pool, bar, restaurant and internet café.

Wildlife Camp, PO Box 53, Mfuwe, tel/fax: (062) 45026, email: info@wildlifecamp-zambia.com, website: www.wildlifecamp-zambia.com Flexible, good value accommodation comprising nine twin/double chalets, two family chalets, a tented camp with five *en-suite* tents overlooking the river, a bushcamp with four twin tents and bucket showers and a campsite; fullboard or self-catering; guided walking safaris and game drives, Kawaza Village tours and overnight village stays.

North Luangwa National Park
Buffalo Camp Shiwa Safaris, tel: (01) 229 261, website: www.shiwasafaris.com Small, rustic camps of reed and thatch, *en-suite* facilities, bucket showers, walks and occasional game drives, excellent guides.

Mwaleshi Camp, Remote Africa Safaris (*see* above). Four reed and thatch chalets, similar facilities and activities to Buffalo Camp.

WHERE TO EAT

Moondog Café, PO Box 100, Mfuwe, tel: (062) 45068, fax: 45025. Handy location next to airport, useful noticeboard for independent travellers, tasty and good value snacks, open May–Dec.

SHOPPING

Magenge Crafts, PO Box 97, Mfuwe, tel: (062) 45094. Located next to Moondog Café, outlet for Tribal Textiles (a community project using local materials), baskets, carvings, wildlife guidebooks.

TOURS AND EXCURSIONS
Mobile Safaris
Operated in the remote north of the park by Robin Pope Safaris following the Mupamadzi River and covering around 10km a day. Up to five days. Maximum group size is six. Available Jun–Sep.

River Safaris
Operated by Tafika Camp (Remote Africa Safaris) canoeing the Luangwa River in full flood. Maximum group size is four. Available Feb–Apr.

Cultural Visits
Overnight visits are possible at **Kawaza Village** (contact Robin Pope Safaris for details). **Nsendamila Cultural Village** is located in the Mfuwe Area. Ask your lodge or camp for information.

MFUWE	J	F	M	A	M	J	J	A	S	O	N	D
AVERAGE TEMP. °F	79	79	79	77	73	68	68	72	77	82	82	81
AVERAGE TEMP. °C	26	26	26	25	23	20	20	22	25	28	28	27
RAINFALL in	7	7	5	2	0	0	0	0	0	1	3	6
RAINFALL mm	190	177	124	60	2	0	0	0	0	19	84	162

6
The Bangweulu Region

Many people are familiar with Botswana's Okavango Delta, the so-called 'Jewel of the Kalahari', but few will even have heard of Zambia's very own water wilderness. Similar in scale to the Okavango, the **Bangweulu Wetlands** sprawl across 9850km² (3800 sq miles) of eastern Zambia. This enormous shallow basin, fed by 17 rivers, has limited tourist facilities. However, those who venture into the vast flood plains and swamps will be rewarded with isolation, infinite horizons, incredible bird life (including the rare **shoebill**) and the chance to spot herds of endemic **black lechwe**.

Another antelope specially adapted to the wetlands is the **sitatunga** – an elusive creature that is best sought in **Kasanka National Park**. This beautiful reserve is on the southeastern edge of the Bangweulu Basin. Despite being one of Zambia's smallest parks, Kasanka boasts a wildlife-rich mixture of river, lake, forest and grassland. Its camps make an ideal base from which to explore the region's other attractions. These include the rock-art site of **Nsalu Cave** and the **Livingstone Memorial** where the famous explorer died during his search for the source of the Nile.

Another extraordinary monument to colonial endeavour lies further north. Completed in 1932, the red-brick manor house of **Shiwa N'gandu** is an impressive, yet incongruous, sight in this remote corner of Zambia. Set in its own, now largely redundant, estate, the house conjures a vivid sense of history and intrigue. Along with Kasanka National Park and the Bangweulu Wetlands, Shiwa N'gandu is one of the region's major attractions.

Opposite: *The aptly named shoebill is a threatened species.*

KASANKA NATIONAL PARK ★★★

Unique in Zambia in that it is managed by an independent charity based in Zambia and the UK, Kasanka National Park covers an area of 390km² (150 sq miles) on the fringe of the Bangweulu Wetlands. Its relatively small size belies a wealth of habitats that are home to abundant wildlife, including rarities like the sitatunga and blue monkey. The bird life is exceptional with 412 species recorded – and the list is still growing.

Visitors can drive their own vehicles around the park or join a game drive from one of the two camps. Kasanka, open year-round, also offers walking safaris, fishing, canoeing and a self-catering camp site.

History

Like most national parks in the region, Kasanka was hard hit by poaching in the 1980s. During a visit to the area in 1985, a British expatriate called David Lloyd heard gunshots and reckoned that if poachers were still firing at animals there must be something left worth saving.

Working with a local farmer, Lloyd began employing game scouts and setting up tourist camps. With government support, they established the Kasanka Trust which, in 1990, was granted permission to manage the park in a way that restored its wildlife and benefited the local community.

Using grants, donations and tourist revenue, the Trust continues to promote sustainable alternatives to poaching in the area. It supports farming and craft projects, as well as other vital community needs, such as education and health. Meanwhile, the national park's wildlife has bounced back. Puku, for example, have increased from a few hundred to over 1500. Kasanka even has a small resident herd of elephant – and more are expected to return to this revitalized sanctuary in the future.

Wildlife

You might expect to find some strange and exotic animals in an African swamp, but few are more beautiful or well adapted to their surroundings than the **sitatunga**. This amphibious antelope, with its striped and spotted coat, has oily, water-repellent fur and splayed hooves which allow it to run, with ease, across spongy areas of marsh. Not only is it a good swimmer, but when alarmed the sitatunga can dive underwater and remain hidden with just its nose above the surface.

   Not surprisingly, many visitors to Kasanka National Park are keen to spot a sitatunga – and they are rarely disappointed. The reserve holds the world's densest and most visible population. Look for them in the papyrus swamp areas.

   Other rewarding habitats to explore in Kasanka include the woodland, which shelters roan and sable antelope, hartebeest, bushpig and yellow baboon. Rivers and lakes contain hippo, crocodile and otter, while adjacent riverine forest is favoured by blue and vervet monkeys.

   Among the **bird** highlights of Kasanka are wattled crane, Pel's fishing owl, African fish eagle, Ross's lourie and several varieties of bee-eater and hornbill.

ACTIVITIES

Safaris and Bird-watching ★★★

A choice of walking safaris, game drives and canoe trips are available in Kasanka National Park. **Walking safaris** can range from a one-hour ramble to a five-day adventure using temporary overnight camps. **Game drives** take place both day and night. You can even drive your own vehicle around the park (during daylight hours only). However, organized game drives have the advantage of excellent visibility from open-top vehicles and the expertise of a local guide. **Canoeing**, meanwhile, is a great way to

Opposite: *The sitatunga, of which only the male has horns, is the most amphibious of the antelopes.*

SAVANNA BABOON

Scientific name:
Papio cynocephalus.
Vital statistics: length, including tail, up to 1.5m (5ft), weight up to 26kg (57lb).
Distinguishing features: stocky build, dog-like muzzle.
Habitat: savanna, woodland fringe.
Diet: everything from grass and roots to insects, bird eggs and newborn antelope.
Breeding: six month gestation, one offspring.
Likes: living in troops, mutual grooming.
Dislikes: leopards, lions, large eagles.

Above: *After burying his heart at this spot in 1873, two of Livingstone's most devout followers, Sussi and Chuma, carried his body to the coast.*
Opposite: *Rock art at Nsalu Caves.*

LAVUSHI MANDA

Covering an area of 1500km² (580 sq miles), **Lavushi Manda National Park** contains an interesting mixture of rugged hills, miombo woodland, riverine forest and grassland. Although there are no roads or tourist facilities inside the park, the Kasanka Trust (*see* page 99) may be able to organize a hike in the area.

---

observe Kasanka's stunning river life. As well as herons, kingfishers and other birds, you may be lucky enough to glimpse a monitor lizard or otter.

During your stay, be sure to visit **Fibwe Hide**, hailed as Africa's best vantage from which to observe the sitatunga antelope. Perched 18m (60ft) off the ground in a giant mahogany tree, the hide's record number of sightings in a single visit is over 90 individuals! As well as sitatunga, Fibwe Hide provides views of another extraordinary wildlife spectacle. Between November and December, a million straw-coloured fruit bats roosting in a nearby area of swamp forest fill the evening sky as they take to the wing on their nightly feeding foray.

Fishing *

With special permits, angling is available in the Luwombwa River, where catches include tiger fish, bream and catfish. Although boats are available for hire, you should bring your own tackle.

EXCURSIONS
Livingstone Memorial **

Located 35km (22 miles) from Kasanka, a simple stone monument marks the spot where Dr David Livingstone's heart was buried in May 1873. When he entered the Bangweulu Wetlands a month earlier, during his obsessive search for the source of the Nile, the explorer was already suffering from malaria and dysentery. He died at Chitambo Village where his followers buried his heart beneath a mupundu tree before carrying his body 1500km (930 miles) to the coast. Livingstone was eventually interred in Westminster Abbey.

The mupundu tree has gone (a section that was engraved with Livingstone's name was shipped to the Royal Geographical Society) and Chitambo Village has also moved. However, Chief Chitambo IV, the great grandson of the chief who received Livingstone shortly before his death, is often willing to meet visitors at his nearby village called Chalilo.

Nsalu Caves ★

This national monument contains rock paintings ranging from 2000 to possibly 100,000 years in age. The older, Stone-Age designs appear as abstract lines and circles. Although somewhat neglected, there are plans to improve the care of this important archaeological site.

Kundalila Falls ★

Cascading 65m (213ft) from the Muchinga Escarpment, the Kundalila, or Crying Dove, Falls lie in a scenic area well-known for its wild flowers. A path leads to a clear pool at the base of the falls where it's possible to take a refreshing swim.

Lake Waka Waka ★

Clear, spring-fed water plus walks in surrounding hills make this a pleasant location for a picnic or overnight camp. Roan and sable antelope are found in the area, but they are nervous and difficult to spot.

CAVES AND FALLS

With a 4x4 vehicle, it is possible to reach Nachikufu Caves and Chipoma Falls, both a relatively short distance from Mpika. The falls are located on the Lubu River to the north of the town, while the caves (which contain rock paintings estimated at around 15,000 years old) can be found about 20km (12 miles) to the south.

BANGWEULU WETLANDS ★★

There is more to Bangweulu than meets the eye. Far from simply being a giant swamp, this internationally important wetland is a dynamic 'water world' pulsing with seasonal floods that spread across the plains east of **Lake Bangweulu**. During the dry season, the waters slowly recede towards the lake until the next rains arrive. Closely attuned to this natural cycle is a plethora of wildlife – vast herds of antelope and a kaleidoscope of water-loving birds – all moving with the ebb and flow of the floods.

Apart from the largely defunct Isangano National Park, there is no formally protected reserve in the heart of the wetlands. Instead, local

SHOEBILL

Scientific name:
Balaeniceps rex.
Vital statistics: height up to 1.2m (4ft).
Distinguishing features: enormous bill, blue/grey plumage.
Habitat: papyrus beds in swamps.
Diet: fish (especially lungfish), frogs, turtles, snakes, lizards.
Breeding: nests on floating mound of reeds.
Likes: going unnoticed while it stalks its prey.
Dislikes: the fact that its habitat is shrinking, making it an endangered species.

communities are being encouraged to act as custodians of their own land inside the Bangweulu Game Management Area. One of their initiatives is **Nsobe**, a small, self-catering tourist camp. The wetlands have only one other camp – an indication, perhaps, of their remoteness.

Wildlife

Try to imagine a dodo on stilts and you will begin to get an idea of what a **shoebill** looks like. This striking stork-like bird, steely blue against a backdrop of papyrus, sports an enormous beak that makes short work of the African lungfish (by no means a tiddler itself). The Bangweulu Wetlands are a crucial refuge for this threatened species – only 1500 may be left – and it's at the top of the list for most bird watchers visiting the area.

Other avian treats include large flocks of wattled crane, both white and pink-backed pelican, spoonbill and Goliath heron. Stalking the plains are ground hornbill, Denham's bustard and crowned crane, while Montagu's and pallid harriers quarter overhead. The shallows positively squirm

with waders and ducks and, if that doesn't satisfy you, try spotting the swamp flycatcher or rosy-breasted longclaw.

Birds aside, the Bangweulu Wetlands are home to 30,000 **black lechwe** – sometimes occurring in herds a thousand strong. This aquatic antelope is endemic to the region, using its powerful hindquarters to propel itself in long leaps across the inundated flood plains. Other antelope present include tsessebe which prefer drier areas near patches of woodland (often growing

Left: *Black lechwe are only found on the flood plains of the Bangweulu Wetlands.*
Opposite: *Local villagers use traditional fishing traps around Lake Bangweulu.*

on termite mounds). Buffalo and elephant occur mainly towards the latter part of the year when the grasslands dry out. Until the 1980s there used to be lion, but you may still encounter other predators like leopard, hyena and jackal during an exceptional night drive.

Activities
Both camps in the area can arrange **boat trips** for **bird-watching** or **fishing**. For the more energetic, **walking safaris** are also available. Flying into the nearby airstrip provides a superb perspective of the seemingly endless flood plains, plus a chance for some **aerial game-viewing**.

SHIWA N'GANDU **
You could be forgiven for thinking you're dreaming as you approach Shiwa N'gandu. Sweeping through the estate's gatehouse, a tree-lined avenue leads to a stately manor house set in formal gardens. There is something disconcertingly English about the scene – it's almost as if a slice of Surrey has been pitched into this far-flung corner of Zambia. Yet, for all its eccentricities, Shiwa N'gandu is a stunning monument to one man's extraordinary vision.

History
In 1914, Stewart Gore-Brown at last found what he was looking for – a piece of land to develop in what was then Northern Rhodesia. He bought 380km² (150 sq miles) bordering Ishiba N'gandu, the Lake of the Royal Crocodile.

KAPISHYA HOT SPRINGS

Located on the estate of Shiwa N'gandu, Kapishya Hot Springs bubble into a crystal-clear pool surrounded by lush vegetation and tall raffia palms before flowing into the Manshya River. A camp site and a cluster of thatched chalets provide the perfect base from which to relax in the springs and visit the nearby manor house.

Above: *The imposing façade of Shiwa N'gandu Manor House.*

INSIDE SHIWA N'GANDU

The interior of Shiwa N'gandu is dusty and atmospheric – a colonial time capsule. Downstairs is a large dining room adorned with Victorian portraits, antelope horns and an elaborate chandelier. The sitting room has leather armchairs and heavy curtains, while an imposing wooden staircase sweeps from the hall to a corridor lined with military prints. The library occupies the central part of the first floor. Packed with leather-bound volumes on military history, philosophy, politics and the classics, the room contains a fireplace with a Latin inscription over the mantelpiece which translates as 'This corner of the earth smiles on me more than any other'.

World War I intervened, but six years later Lt-Col Gore-Brown returned to his renamed Shiwa N'gandu with big plans. Employing and training a huge local workforce, he began building an estate complete with workers' cottages, school, medical clinic and workshops. In 1927, his young English wife, Lorna, joined him and by 1932 the manor house was completed – all built from local materials, but filled with furniture, ornaments and cutlery shipped from England.

They experimented with various crops before focussing on citrus fruits as a profitable source of income for the estate. Tragically a virus killed the fruit trees in the 1950s, forcing Shiwa N'gandu to revert to less profitable forms of agriculture.

Always active in politics, Gore-Brown made a positive contribution to Zambia's independence. Knighted by King George VI, he died (aged 84) in 1967 and was buried on a hill overlooking his beloved Lake of the Royal Crocodile – an honour usually reserved for Bemba chiefs.

Today, Shiwa N'gandu is run by Gore-Brown's grandson, Charlie Harvey and his wife. Since moving here in 2001 from their farm near Chisamba, they have revitalized the place. It is now a thriving estate, employing up to 200 people and supporting 1200 cattle, 900 sheep and a well-stocked game farm.

The Bangweulu Region at a Glance

Kasanka National Park is open year-round. Bird-watching is particularly good during the wet season, **Nov–Mar**, while game-viewing is best from **May–Oct**. In the Bangweulu Wetlands, the flood waters usually start receding by **Apr–May** making it possible to use 4x4 vehicles for close-up views of black lechwe. In **Jun–Jul** walking safaris are available. Bird-watching is excellent all year, although enthusiasts may want to visit during the wet summer months when migrants are present.

Kasanka National Park has an airstrip which can handle light aircraft **charter flights**. Alternatively, you can **drive** from Lusaka on good roads via Kapiri Moshi and Serenje. To reach the Bangweulu Wetlands by road demands an adventurous 12hr journey from Lusaka, the latter half through remote areas requiring at least two 4x4 vehicles, ample experience, time and fuel! There is also an airstrip at the edge of the wetlands, but bear in mind that access to Bangweulu is largely dictated by the flood waters. Most visitors leave it to the experts and arrange a package which combines visits to Kasanka, Bangweulu and Shiwa N'gandu.

Kasanka National Park
MID-RANGE
Wasa Lodge,
Kasanka Trust, PO Box 850073, Serenje, satellite tel: (00873) 762 067 959, email: trust@kasanka.com, website: www.kasanka.com Beautiful lakeside position, three *en-suite* rondavels and six simpler chalets, main lodge building with bar and dining room. Can arrange visits to nearby attractions (Livingstone Memorial etc) as well as activities in the national park, from canoeing to fishing.

MID-RANGE/BUDGET
Luwombwa Lodge, Kasanka Trust (see above). Five chalets, some with four beds, riverside location, superb birdwatching. Campsites with simple toilets, showers and shelters available.

Bangweulu Wetlands
MID-RANGE/BUDGET
Shoebill Island Camp, book through Kasanka Trust. Six reed and thatch chalets with *en-suite* showers and toilets, superb position for exploring the wetlands by boat or drier areas by vehicle or on foot.

BUDGET
Nsobe Safari Camp,
booking in advance is difficult but try: PO Box 450141, Chiundaponde, Mpika, or c/o WWF Wetlands Project, tel: (01) 278231. Community-run camp, five chalets, simple facilities, game-viewing activities by foot, boat and vehicle.

Shiwa N'gandu
LUXURY/MID-RANGE
Shiwa N'gandu Manor House, PO Box 1, Shiwa N'gandu, Mpika, tel: (04) 370 134, website: www.shiwangandu.com Five *en-suite* rooms, try 'The Africa House'.

MID-RANGE
Kapishya Hot Springs, book through Shiwa Safaris (see page 89) Five-chalet lodge on Shiwa N'gandu Estate, self-catering kitchen, camp site with running water, toilets and hot showers, river trips, guided walks, tours of Shiwa N'gandu, game-viewing, fishing and horseriding.

Three waterfalls can be visited in the Shiwa/Kapishya region. Self-drive is possible, but its easier to locate them with a guide. Chusa Falls is a 10km drive from Kapishya, the best option for a day trip, while the Senkele Falls and (most impressively) the double Namudela Falls lie further afield.

MPIKA	J	F	M	A	M	J	J	A	S	O	N	D
AVERAGE TEMP. ºF	70	70	70	68	64	63	61	64	70	73	73	70
AVERAGE TEMP. ºC	21	21	21	20	18	17	16	18	21	23	23	21
RAINFALL in	9	9	6	1	0	0	0	0	0	0	4	10
RAINFALL mm	239	230	164	39	5	0	0	0	2	10	94	255

7
Northern Zambia

Surrounded on three sides by Malawi, Tanzania and the Democratic Republic of the Congo (DRC), Northern Zambia is a land of extremes. Here you will find the country's deepest waters and its highest mountains – both providing cool respite after the hot Luangwa and Zambezi valleys.

Although Zambia lays claim to only seven per cent of its total surface area of around 34,000km² (13,100 sq miles), **Lake Tanganyika** still appears as an inland sea lapping at the country's northern tip. It is the world's longest freshwater lake and its second deepest – plummeting to 1433m (4700ft). Nearby is the dramatic plume of **Kalambo Falls**, the second tallest on the continent. Renowned for superb **angling**, Lake Tanganyika borders on one of the region's most popular reserves, the **Sumbu National Park**. Although not as richly endowed as Zambia's more famous parks, Sumbu contains a good range of mammals and birds in a beautiful wilderness setting.

Further west, towards the border with the DRC, determined travellers can probe routes leading to **Lake Mweru**, as well as various **waterfalls** on the Luapula and Kalungwishi rivers.

However, besides Lake Tanganyika and Sumbu National Park, the region's other main highlight is the **Nyika Plateau**. Straddling the border between Zambia and Malawi, this spectacular highland soars to over 2500m (8200ft) in places. The plateau's undulating grassland supports a variety of plants and animals, including rare orchids and an endemic race of zebra. **Hiking** and

DON'T MISS

★★★ Nyika Plateau: remote highland best visited from Malawi, but worth the effort for its contrasts with the rest of Zambia.
★★ Sumbu National Park: water sports and angling on Lake Tanganyika.
★★ Kalambo Falls: graceful waterfall reached after a short hike.
★ Mpulungu: The only port in Zambia.

Opposite: *Vibrant colours and patterns adorn a materials stall at Mpulungu Market.*

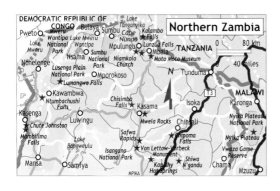

horse riding are the best ways to explore the park, which involves a short detour into Malawi for the easiest access.

LAKE TANGANYIKA ★★

In a country like Zambia, it's all too easy to become slightly obsessed with large, charismatic wildlife like elephant, lion and buffalo. Lake Tanganyika provides the perfect excuse to praise some of the country's more obscure species – namely fish.

Even the most ardent 'big five' enthusiast could not fail to be impressed by the fishy credentials of this inland sea lying in the southern reaches of the Great Rift Valley. Not only is it home to over 450 different species, but most are found nowhere else. This extraordinary level of endemicity is thought to be due to the lake's great age and isolation. Scientists believe that the lifeless water at the bottom of the lake may be 20 million years old. By contrast, the surface layers are constantly being stirred by winds – providing the oxygen-rich water that fish need.

Important commercial and sports fishing species include giant Nile perch, Goliath tiger fish, Lake Tanganyika yellow belly and kapenta. Popular with aquarists is a diverse and colourful group known as cichlids – 98 per cent of which are unique to the lake. Also endemic are the lake's seven species of crabs and half of its molluscs. Fortunately, a project has been established to maintain Tanganyika's biodiversity.

Mpulungu ★

Zambia's only port, Mpulungu is a busy fishing base and a stop-off for the ferry, *MV Liemba*, which plies Lake Tanganyika. There are a few shoreline lodges nearby which can arrange **snorkelling** and **fishing trips**, as well as visits to nearby attractions.

TANGANYIKA FERRY

The *MV Liemba* is one of two ferries serving Mpulungu on its regular circuit of Lake Tanganyika. Originally a cargo ship in German-occupied Tanganyika (now Tanzania), it was used as a military vessel against British forces in Northern Rhodesia during World War I. Bombed in 1916, it was salvaged and transported to Kigoma before taking on a new lease of life as a passenger and cargo vessel. The *MV Liemba* has cabins with bunk beds, as well as a restaurant and bar serving simple meals and drinks.

Safety

Although the beaches are sandy and the water clear and inviting, swimmers should be aware that localized groups of hippo and crocodile inhabit the lake. Rare cases of bilharzia may also occur and there are occasional sightings of a swimming snake called the Tanganyika cobra. Don't be put off – just seek local advice before taking a dip.

Niamkolo Church ★

Built in 1895 by the London Missionary Society, a 15m (50ft) tower is all that remains of Zambia's oldest surviving church, located 2km (1.25 miles) east of Mpulungu.

Kalambo Falls ★★

At 221m (725ft), Kalambo Falls are over twice the height of Victoria Falls, but considerably narrower! A cliff-top path provides excellent views of both the waterfall and Lake Tanganyika. Look out for a nesting colony of marabou storks in the gorge and palmnut vultures circling overhead. Kalambo Falls is a celebrated archaeological site – the first evidence of human-made fire south of the Sahara was found here, along with stone tools over 100,000 years old.

Moto Moto Museum ★

Located near Mbala, south of Mpulungu, this national museum exhibits a variety of cultural and local artefacts from the area, including prehistoric findings from Kalambo

> ### TANGANYIKA CICHLIDS
>
> A diverse family of freshwater fish, cichlids range in size from the golden emperor cichlid, weighing up to 3.5kg (7.7 lb), to the diminutive zebra cichlid, no larger than a thumbnail. Cichlids have evolved an extraordinary range of feeding techniques, including algae-grazing, scale-nipping and even cannibalism. Their breeding habits are no less bizarre. Many use empty shells for protection, while some employ a method known as mouth-brooding, in which the female gathers up the eggs in her mouth. Even once they've hatched, the cichlid fry retreat to their parent's mouth when danger threatens.

Left: *Sheltered by a large offshore island, Mpulungu is located around a bay on Lake Tanganyika's southern shore.*

Above: *Comprising metre-thick sandstone walls, the tower of Niamkolo Church was once used as a landmark for boats visiting the port of Mpulungu.*

Falls. Also on display are the flag and propeller of the *SS Good News*, a 16m (54ft) missionary steamboat which was launched on Lake Tanganyika in 1895 after a momentous journey from the mouth of the Zambezi River.

SUMBU NATIONAL PARK ★★

Covering an area of some 2020km^2 (780 sq miles), Sumbu National Park is perhaps better known for its angling than wildlife-viewing. Three lodges, located in bays along the park's pristine section of Tanganyika's shoreline, offer fishing enthusiasts direct access to the lake. Local Tabwa fishermen make offerings to the Spirit of the Lake at a sacred place just east of the park. Cape Nundo, within Sumbu's boundaries, is another revered site. Strange balancing boulders are the focus for an annual ceremony in which a white chicken is sacrificed.

Wildlife

Although still recovering from the effects of poaching, Sumbu National Park supports a variety of **mammals**, including elephant, buffalo, zebra, lion and leopard. Nkamba Bay Lodge have built special hides from which patient observers may glimpse the shy sitatunga antelope. The park is also home to roan and sable antelopes, as well as eland, Lichtenstein's hartebeest, waterbuck, reedbuck and puku. The diminutive blue duiker, a secretive forest species weighing as little as 4kg (9lb), is one of Sumbu's specialities.

One of the more unusual avian visitors to Sumbu National Park, which lies under the flight path of migrating **birds**, is the flamingo. During boat trips look out for whiskered tern, grey-headed gull and the African skimmer which, as the name implies, skims the water surface for food using the extended lower mandible of its bill. Other shoreline birds include storks, ducks, herons and, of course, the ubiquitous African fish eagle. Further inland, you will spot many species typical of Zambian parks. However, one or two of Sumbu's birds are more commonly found in East Africa. Perhaps the most conspicuous are the bare-faced go-away bird and small flocks of the finch-like red-cheeked cordon bleu.

ACTIVITIES

As well as **game drives** and **walks**, the lodges in the area offer **lake cruises** and night-time visits to the **kapenta fishing rigs**. One or two can even organize **water-skiing**, **snorkelling** and **scuba diving** – but check the local crocodile and hippo situation first.

Fishing **

Sumbu National Park is renowned for its catches of Nile perch, Goliath tiger fish, vundu catfish, golden perch and yellow belly. Boat hire is widely available, although most anglers bring their own rods and tackle. One of the most sought-after challenges is the Goliath tiger fish which can weigh around 40kg (88lb). It is found in very deep water and can be lured with fish fillet, spoons and spinners. Each March or April, the annual Zambian National Fishing Competition is held at Kasaba Bay. Records are frequently broken.

VON LETTOW VORBECK

If driving on the main road between Mpika and Kasama, keep an eye open for a monument at the north end of the bridge that spans the Chambeshi River. It marks the spot where General Von Lettow Vorbeck, commander of the German forces in East Africa during World War 1, surrendered to Hector Croad, the British District Commissioner, on 14 November 1918. The monument incorporates a German breach-loading field gun that was used in the campaign.

Below: *Local fishermen haul nets from the teeming waters of Lake Tanganyika.*

LUAPULA WATERFALLS

The Luapula River flows north into Lake Mweru, following Zambia's border with the southeast corner of the Democratic Republic of the Congo. For the adventurous traveller there are several picturesque and rarely visited waterfalls in the area, including Mambilima Falls, Mumbuluma Falls and Musonda Falls.

Below: *A horse-riding safari camp on the high grasslands of the Nyika Plateau.*

THE CONGO BORDER ★

Tourist facilities are few and far between as you travel towards northern Zambia's border with the Democratic Republic of the Congo (DRC), and visitors should check the political situation before venturing here. There are two national parks – Mweru Wantipa and Lusenga Plain – but neither are particularly worth visiting. Poaching has decimated their wildlife and they have little or no visitor infrastructure. The area's main attractions are **Lake Mweru** and several nearby waterfalls – particularly **Lumangwe Falls** and **Ntumbachushi Falls**.

Before a surfaced road existed in the lakeside village of **Nchelenge** in 1987, much of Lake Mweru's shore was sparsely populated. Now it is home to several communities thriving on the lake's rich fishing grounds. Accommodation in Nchelenge is limited to a couple of simple guesthouses and there is also a boat service to the islands of Kilwa and Isokwe.

Flowing into Lake Mweru from the east, the Kalungwishi River nurtures the spectacular and little-known Lumangwe Falls. Measuring 100m (330ft) across and 40m (130ft) high, this rainbow-filled cascade has been likened to a miniature Victoria Falls. It is located near the Chimpembe pontoon on the road between Kawambwa and Mporokoso.

Further south are the Ntumbachushi Falls, a series of pools and rapids culminating in the main cascade of about 30m (98ft) in height.

THE NYIKA PLATEAU ★★★

Only 80km² (31 sq miles) in area, Zambia's Nyika Plateau National Park adjoins a much larger protected area across the border in Malawi. Access to this beautiful highland region of undulating grassland dissected by deep valleys is best made from Malawi's Nyika National Park which covers around

3100km² (1200 sq miles). From Zambia, you can drive there in a normal vehicle during the dry season. However, the easiest way to reach the plateau is to fly to the Chilinda airstrip located in the heart of Nyika National Park.

Above: *Reminiscent of a mini-Victoria Falls, Lumangwe Falls is far less visited.*

Wildlife

The rolling green swathes of the Nyika Plateau support a wide variety of **mammals**, including herds of an endemic race of Burchell's zebra. Red duiker, reedbuck, bushbuck, eland and herds of up to 300 roan antelope are also regularly seen, along with warthog and scrub hare. At lower elevations, where grassland gives way to woodland, elephant and buffalo may be encountered. Night drives promise glimpses of a nocturnal cast of creatures, such as leopard, serval, civet, genet, hyena, honey badger, bushbaby and porcupine.

The majority of Nyika's 435 **bird** species are found in the densely wooded foothills, and include rarities like the cinnamon dove and bar-tailed trogon. More conspicuous grassland species to watch out for include Denham's bustard, wattled crane and ground hornbill. Pacing the grassland in search of rodents, snakes, insects and other prey, ground hornbills can walk up to 11km (7 miles) a day. These magnificent birds are easily recognized by their black plumage and huge downward curving bills. Adults call to each other with a low-pitched booming – a mesmerizing sound that is guaranteed to halt you in your tracks.

During such a pause be sure to have a good look at the ground. The Nyika Plateau is renowned for its **wild flowers**. Around 200 varieties of orchid grow here, including several that are unique to the area. October and November signal the start of a spectacular floral display. Gladioli, pelargoniums, hibiscus and everlasting flowers are some of the first to bloom, followed by proteas and giant lobelias.

WARTHOG

Scientific name: *Phacochoerus africanus.*
Vital statistics: length up to 1.3m (4ft), weight up to 100kg (220lb).
Distinguishing features: curved tusks, tail held erect when alarmed.
Habitat: savannas, flood plains, woodland.
Diet: grass, fruit, bark, roots.
Breeding: 5½-month gestation period, litter of 2–4 born at start of the rainy season.
Likes: dust-bathing and mud-wallowing.
Dislikes: lion, leopard and cheetah.

Below: *Horse riding is
an exhilarating way to
experience the Nyika
Plateau and encounter
its varied wildlife.*

ACTIVITIES
Hiking ★★★

Although driving is an excellent way to appreciate Nyika's
wildlife and dramatic scenery, the plateau also offers
superb walking country. It is generally cool and perfectly
safe to set out on foot and there is a variety of hiking
options to choose from.

With a vehicle you can reach the starting points of several short walks visiting some of the park's highlights. These
include **Nganda Peak**, the highest point on the plateau at
2605m (8547ft); **Jalawe Rock**, with its stunning panorama
of mountain, lake and forest; and **Fingira Rock**, a 3000-
year-old human settlement site with rock paintings.

Longer hikes, ranging from one to five nights, are also
possible. There are six **wilderness trails** and you will
need to hire an armed game scout and carry your own
camping equipment and food. The most popular trail
takes three days from Chelinda to Livingstonia Mission
on the eastern side of the park. It crosses some beautiful
grassland before descending steeply through the
Mwenembwe Forest.

Horse Riding ★★

Both novice and experienced riders can explore the Nyika
Plateau on horseback.
Riding not only provides
a wonderful vantage
point from which to
admire the scenery, but
it is often possible to
approach wildlife much
closer than on foot.
Imagine the exhilaration
of trotting alongside
herds of eland and
zebra! Horseback trails
range from a morning's
introduction to a fully
supported camping safari
lasting a week or more.

Northern Zambia at a Glance

Sumbu National Park is open **year-round**. The annual fishing competition takes place here around **Mar/Apr**.
On the Nyika Plateau the cool, dry season is **May–Oct**. The main rains fall on Nyika from **Jan–Feb**.

Lake Tanganyika
A main **road** leads from Lusaka to Mpulungu on the shores of Lake Tanganyika from where **water taxis** serve the lodges in Sumbu National Park. Alternatively, there are **flights** from Lusaka and Ndola to Kasaba Bay Lodge inside the park. Mpulungu is served by **ferry** from Kigoma in Tanzania and Bujumbura in Burundi.

Nyika Plateau
Access is from Malawi. During the dry season it is possible to drive a **standard vehicle** via Chipata and Lundazi, crossing the border to Mzimba and Mzuzu before going on to Nyika National Park in Malawi. A **4x4** is needed for this in the wet season. Regular **flights** are from Lilongwe to Mzuzu and on to Chelinda Lodge.

Boats are available for hire at lodges in Sumbu National Park. Other organized activities include game drives and walks. Nyika Plateau is best explored on foot or **horseback**.

Mpulungu
BUDGET
Mishembe Bay, reached by water taxi from Mpulungu, tel/fax: (04) 221 615. Lovely beach setting, self-catering chalets and camp site, guided walks to Kalambo Falls.
Nkupi Lodge, located on the edge of town, tel: (04) 455 166. Basic clean chalets, camp site, boats for hire.

Sumbu National Park
LUXURY
Kasaba Bay Lodge, Naturelink, PO Box 15585, Sinoville, 0129, South Africa, tel: (27 12) 543 3448, fax: 543 9110, e-mail: nature link@mweb.co.za Thirteen *en-suite* thatched chalets overlooking the lake, there are boats for hire, cruises and game drives.

MID-RANGE/BUDGET
Ndole Bay Lodge, PO Box 21033, Kitwe, tel: (02) 711 150, fax: 711 390, e-mail: ndolebay@coppernet.zm Just outside park, attractive lodge, 13 comfortable chalets, camp site, game drives, walks, fishing, snorkelling and water-skiing.

Nyika Plateau
Chelinda Lodge and **Chelinda Camp**, The Nyika Safari Company, PO Box 1006, Mzuzu, tel: (265) 133 0180, e-mail: reservations@nyika.com website: www.nyika.com
Chelinda Lodge: stunning location at 2100m (6890ft), eight *en-suite* twin-bed log cabins with open fires, comfortable lounge, excellent food.
Chelinda Camp: six *en-suite* twin-bed rooms, four self-catering cottages, camp site. Game drives, walking safaris, horse riding, fishing, mountain biking and local excursions. A camp site with hot showers and toilets is located 1.5km away.

Nyika Plateau
Chelinda Lodge can arrange overnight **walking safaris** from 2–5 nights, led by a guide and using tents. Independent hikers can tackle **wilderness trails** if accompanied by an armed game scout and prepared to carry food and equipment.
Horseback safaris – limited to eight riders escorted by a guide. Short daily forays from Chelinda or a week-long safari for experienced riders, Mar–Dec.

KASAMA	J	F	M	A	M	J	J	A	S	O	N	D
AVERAGE TEMP. °F	70	70	70	70	68	64	63	66	72	75	73	70
AVERAGE TEMP. °C	21	21	21	21	20	18	17	19	22	24	23	21
RAINFALL in	11	10	11	3	1	0	0	0	0	1	6	9
RAINFALL mm	272	252	277	71	13	0	0	0	0	20	163	241

8
Western Zambia

A wilderness to yourself? In western Zambia this might not sound like such a far-fetched notion. Dominated by vast flood plains and unbroken swathes of woodland, this remote region offers intrepid travellers a taste of Africa.

Although **Kafue National Park** has several camps and lodges, it is also one of the world's largest nature reserves and tourists are not a common sight. The same cannot be said for its abundant and diverse wildlife which includes Serengeti-style herds of antelope in the **Busanga Plains**. Flooded and inaccessible for half the year, this spectacular northern section of the park is a challenge to reach – usually requiring a light aircraft flight, followed by a bumpy ride in a 4x4 vehicle to a seasonal bush camp.

More adventures await travellers to the far west of Zambia. Here, you will find other even more isolated parks and reserves. The tiny **Nchila Wildlife Reserve**, situated close to the source of the Zambezi River, has a small bush camp, while visitors to **West Lunga National Park** will need to be determined, experienced and totally self-sufficient.

Liuwa Plain National Park is one of Zambia's most pristine and little-visited reserves. It is here that one of Africa's last great undisturbed wildlife spectacles takes place when, each October and November, thousands of wildebeest, zebra and buffalo begin their migration across the grasslands.

Beyond the national parks, western Zambia also offers glimpses of traditional rural life in areas such as **Barotseland**. In addition there is superb angling on the **Upper Zambezi River**, while adrenaline-seekers can raft the rapids below **Ngonye Falls**.

DON'T MISS

★★★ Kafue National Park: enormous wilderness reserve, renowned for its antelope.
★★★ Busanga Plains: wildlife-rich flood plain in the Kafue National Park, only accessible during the dry season.
★★ Barotseland: scene of the annual Ku-omboka ceremony in which the Lozi people migrate to higher ground.
★★ Liuwa Plain National Park: remote but spectacular reserve hosting impressive wildebeest migration.
★★ Ngonye Falls: notable horse-shoe falls on the Zambezi River.

Opposite: *Leopards are adept tree-climbers, as this one demonstrates.*

KAFUE CAMPS

Like all of Zambia's major national parks, Kafue has a good choice of camps and lodges offering remarkably high standards of comfort in a wilderness setting. If you are averse to a little pampering, however, there is also a handful of self-catering camp sites – though *not* in Busanga Plains.

KAFUE NATIONAL PARK ★★★

Kafue is huge. At 22,400km² (8646 sq miles), it is similar in size to Wales or the US state of New Hampshire. Not only is it Zambia's largest national park (over twice the size of South Luangwa), but it also ranks in the top five of Africa's biggest nature reserves.

However, despite its size, Kafue National Park was not immune to the impact of poaching during the 1980s. Black rhinoceros were eradicated, while some elephant herds remain shy and elusive. Nevertheless, Kafue's wildlife has generally made a strong recovery, flushing the flood plains, river channels and mopane woodland with a fantastic array of big game.

To get the most out of a visit to Kafue, try to spend a few days in both the northern and southern sections of the park. With their big skies and uncluttered horizons, the **Busanga Plains** in the far north are a complete contrast to more wooded areas further south. From the vantage of a termite mound, you really can see the curve of the earth!

Busanga has been compared to the Serengeti – herds of antelope and zebra pepper the grassland, while every shady spot seems to have a pride of dozing lions. What makes this region particularly special, however, is the life-giving pulse of annual floods. Lechwe, sitatunga and hippo thrive in both the seasonally inundated plains and year-round swamps. In April, when the floods recede, fresh grass attracts thousands of grazing animals – and their predators are never far behind.

Below: *Buffalo stream across the grasslands of Busanga Plains in the remote north of Kafue National Park.*

In the far south of the park is another open area, known as the **Nanzhila Plains**, a wildlife-rich mosaic of grassland and tree-crowned termite mounds. Nearby, the dammed **Lake Itezhi Tezhi** covers an area of 370km² (140 sq miles). It's a favoured spot for hippos, while drowned trees along its shoreline provide roosting and breeding sites for water birds such as cormorants and the African fish eagle.

Wildlife

If you are a fan of **antelopes**, Kafue National Park will keep you riveted. It supports at least 16 species, including sitatunga, red lechwe, blue wildebeest, Lichtenstein's hartebeest, reedbuck, oribi, puku, impala, roan, sable, kudu, bushbuck, eland, common duiker, grysbok and defassa waterbuck. This impressive line-up is proof of Kafue's diversity of habitats. Antelopes have evolved to live almost anywhere – in Kafue you will find the amphibious, swamp-dwelling sitatunga, the fleet-hoofed impala of the plains, and the tiny, skittish duiker of scrub and woodland.

Adaptations aside, however, Kafue may well be your best chance in Zambia to spot the splendid sable antelope. This handsome beast, with its long, swept-back horns, is usually found in scattered woodland. Family herds can number 40 individuals, but look out for the smaller bachelor groups of up to 10 males – with their glossy black coats, snowy bellies and scimitar horns they are surely one of wild Africa's most striking sights.

With such an abundance of antelope on the menu (not to mention zebra and buffalo), **predators** are widespread in Kafue. Lion prides of up to 20 individuals are not uncommon on the Busanga Plains. There is another big cat present in the park, however, which many visitors will be keen to spot. Kafue's large plains are one of the few areas in Zambia where cheetah are regularly seen. Reaching 112kph (70mph), the cheetah's speed and hunting prowess is legendary.

Considerably slower across the plains, but nevertheless another record holder, is the kori bustard – the world's heaviest flying bird. It is sometimes spotted strutting across Busanga Plains, and is just one of around 450 **bird** species found in the national park. Unless you are particularly

ON THE MOVE

African Experience (see page 120) can arrange two-day canoeing safaris on the Lunga River, camping overnight with simple bucket-shower and bush-toilet facilities. They also run week-long mobile safaris with an emphasis on either walking or canoeing. Nights are spent in basic fly camps, as well as Lunga Lodge and Busanga Bush Camp.

Kafue National Park

inspired to seek out cisticolas, larks and other 'little brown jobs', the grassland's main avian rewards are large birds like wattled crane, secretary bird and saddle-billed stork. For more variety, head to the rivers and pools where you will soon be ticking off kingfishers, bee-eaters, skimmers, ducks and, if you're exceptionally lucky, a rarity like the African finfoot or Pel's fishing owl.

How to Visit

Although it is possible to travel overland to Kafue National Park, many visitors shun the rough tracks in favour of a fly-in safari. Small, single-propeller aircraft can probe the most remote airstrips where 4x4 safari vehicles will be waiting to transport you into the heart of this extraordinary wilderness park.

ACTIVITIES
Game Drives ★★★

Lodges and camps scattered throughout Kafue National Park provide early morning and late afternoon game drives. Be sure also to take advantage of any night drives on offer. There is something particularly magical about travelling through the dark expanse of the Busanga Plains, your eyes fixed to the roving beam of a spotlight, never quite sure what you'll see next. It could be a nightjar, fluttering from the track like a giant, wind-tossed moth, or a brief glimpse of a scrub hare bounding for cover. Even if you see nothing more, you'll be mesmerized by the strange percussion of an African night – the trilling of a pearl-spotted owl, the ratchet clicks of frogs, and the distant roar of a lion carrying from far across the plains.

Below: *The open grass-lands of Liuwa Plain provide excellent hunting territory for the cheetah.*

Walking Safaris ★★

For bird-watchers and those interested in animal track-ing, a walking safari is highly recommended. Prime spots include watercourses where a variety of habitats

are likely to be condensed into a small area. A word of advice: tsetse flies can be a nuisance in the woodland areas of the park, so keep covered up and use insect repellent whether walking or driving.

Fishing ★

Bream, barbel and pike are found in the Kafue River and its tributaries, while Lake Itezhi Tezhi also provides fishing possibilities.

Above: *Lodges near Lake Itezhi Tezhi provide a good base from which to explore the southern parts of Katue National Park.*

THE FAR WEST

Three main roads lead to the far west of Zambia. One threads through the Copperbelt towards the northern out-post town of Mwinilunga; another connects Lusaka with Mongu; and the third follows the Zambezi from Livingstone towards Sesheke and beyond. Don't, however, be lulled into thinking that this is an easy area to get around in. The national parks and other highlights of the far west are notoriously difficult to access, often requiring 4x4 vehicles, bush flights or a combination of both.

Nchila Wildlife Reserve ★★

At just over 40km² (15 sq miles) in area, Nchila Wildlife Reserve, tucked into the extreme northwest of Zambia, may seem a long way to go for such a diminutive spot on the map. But those who do get this far will gain a fascinating insight into a beautiful and sensitively run reserve. Several species of antelope have been reintro-duced to Nchila's mixture of woodland and dambo. Traditional footpaths through the reserve have been respected and maintained, while the reserve's small self-catering guesthouse has been constructed using local labour and materials. Nchila's bird list is impressive. The reserve supports species more typical of nearby Angola

---

LION

Scientific name: *Panthera leo.*
Vital statistics: length, including tail, up to 4.3m (14ft), weight up to 240kg (530lb).
Distinguishing features: large size, tawny colour and long tail.
Habitat: savanna, flood plain, woodland.
Diet: everything from tortoises to giraffes, mainly medium–large antelope, buffalo, zebra.
Breeding: gestation period of 3½ months, 1–4cubs.
Likes: dozing under trees during the heat of the day.
Dislikes: adolescent males which have outgrown the pride.

Right: *Common through-out Zambia, the vervet monkey is an opportunist, eating anything from fruit to fledglings.*

and the DRC – but provides a politically more stable environment in which to see them.

West Lunga National Park

This one is strictly for ardent 4x4 enthusiasts! There are no facilities whatsoever in West Lunga National Park, and you will need to travel with several vehicles in case one gets stuck or breaks down.

Liuwa Plain National Park ★★★

A golden sea of grass, abundant wildlife and very few visitors. Liuwa Plain National Park sounds irresistible – but there's a catch. Not only is it extremely remote, but the entire reserve, covering 3660km² (1413 sq miles), is founded on soft Kalahari sand, making access extremely difficult. In the past, even experienced mobile safari operators have had difficulty trying to reach the area. In October 2000, the first permanent camp was established, but this no longer exists and the only way to visit the park is to organize your own 4WD expedition or join a fly-in safari with Royal Barotse Safaris.

Barotseland **

One of the most culturally fascinating parts of Zambia, the Barotse flood plains of the Zambezi River are home to the cattle-farming Lozi. Their king is known as the Litunga and each year, towards the end of the rainy season, he leads his people from Lealui to higher ground in order to escape the annual flood waters. This traditional migration, dating back some 300 years, is heralded by the **Ku-omboka ceremony** (*see* page 24). Drums signal that the time has come to pack belongings into canoes and follow the Litunga in his royal barge to the Lozi's wet season capital, Limulunga. Once there, the Lozi celebrate the move with feasting, singing and dancing.

Most tourists travelling to Barotseland will eventually find themselves in **Mongu**, one of the district's main towns with banks, fuel stations, shops and a few small hotels. Nearby is the **Nayuma Museum** which houses interesting exhibits on Lozi craft and culture. North of Mongu is a spattering of **fishing camps** which are renowned for excellent tiger fishing on the upper reaches of the Zambezi.

Visit around late October or November, when dramatic rainstorms unleash a floral frenzy around the sandy pans, and you may be lucky enough to witness what many regard as one of Africa's last great undisturbed animal migrations. Thousands of blue wildebeest arrive from Angola to give birth on the rejuvenated grassland in the company of zebra, buffalo and tsessebe. Other resident

Below: *Many camps and lodges in Zambia go to great lengths to preserve their natural surroundings.*

WATTLED CRANE

Scientific name:
Grus carunculata.
Vital statistics: height up to 1.2m (4ft).
Distinguishing features: wattles hanging on either side of chin.
Habitat: open grassland, flood plain.
Diet: frogs, insects, tubers.
Breeding: large grass nest on ground, 1–2 chicks.
Likes: performing wild courtship dance, jumping and tossing grass in the air.
Dislikes: the fact that it is a threatened species.

Below: *The royal barge leads the spectacular Lozi river parade of the Ku-omboka ceremony.*

herbivores include particularly abundant oribi, large herds of red lechwe and roan antelope.

Lion and cheetah make the most of this seasonal influx of prey and you may even be fortunate enough to encounter a pack of wild dogs. These beautiful, though much persecuted, carnivores have a patchwork coat of black, white and ochre. Another strikingly marked hunter of Liuwa Plain is the serval – a spotted cat with an extraordinary ability to locate and pounce on rodents hidden in the grass.

The park supports at least 300 bird species. Grassland is prime strutting ground for the secretary bird, Stanley's bustard and large flocks of both crowned and wattled cranes. Birds of prey, like the formidable marshall eagle with its 2m (6.5ft) wingspan, are widespread. During the wet season, water-filled pans attract pelicans, egrets, ducks and storks.

Ngonye Falls **

Although overshadowed by Victoria Falls further downstream, Ngonye Falls is still a spectacular sight – particularly

during the first half of the year when flood waters nourish the 20m (65ft) high horseshoe falls.

The best **viewpoint** is from directly in front of the falls, either from a small island or from a boat trip organized by nearby Maziba Bay Lodge. Alternatively, you can hire the lodge's **microlight** for a bird's-eye view. Maziba Bay also runs **whitewater rafting** trips on the rapids below Ngonye Falls. The thrills and spills are less intense here than at Victoria Falls, but Ngonye's rapids will still get your pulse racing. For something equally spirited, head south towards Sesheke where there are one or two **fishing camps** on the banks of the Zambezi River renowned for tiger fish.

Above: *Ngonye Falls (also known as Sioma Falls) is located 300km (186 miles) upstream of Victoria Falls and offers a stretch of grade 3 whitewater rafting.*

Sioma Ngwezi National Park ★

Wedged against the borders of Angola and Namibia, Sioma Ngwezi National Park covers an area of around 5000km² (1930 sq miles). It is another of Zambia's remote and seldom-visited parks with no permanent facilities and few roads. However, all this might change in the future. Sioma Ngwezi is well positioned to tempt tourists from the Livingstone/Victoria Falls area. And with proper management its wildlife could recover from poaching. As well as elephant (which migrate back and forth across the Zambezi), Sioma Ngwezi is home to giraffe, lion, cheetah, wild dog and several species of antelope.

Western Zambia at a Glance

Due to seasonal flooding in the north of Kafue National Park, lodges and camps here are open from **Jun/Jul–Nov**. In the southern half of the park, accommodation is available year-round – although heavy summer rains can make access difficult. Nchila Wildlife Reserve is open **May–Dec**. The wildebeest migration usually arrives in Liuwa Plain National Park by **mid/late Oct** and moves north again after the rainy season. The park's camp closes from **Jan–Apr**. Ngonye Falls are worth viewing at any time of the year, although whitewater rafting is best from **Feb–May**.

Kafue National Park
Due to its huge size and difficult roads most visitors take a **light aircraft** to the park, followed by a transfer to their lodge or camp by **4x4 safari vehicle**. As a rough guide, charter flights from Livingstone and Lusaka take 1–2hr to reach airstrips in the park. Driving to Kafue *is* possible and can be a rewarding adventure. However, it is best done as an organized trip – unless you have the experience and time to equip your own 4x4 mini-expedition.

The Far West
Nchila Wildlife Reserve can be reached by **charter flight** from Lusaka and Kafue National

Park, or a lengthy **drive** across and beyond the Copperbelt. Mongu is served by **buses** and **flights** from Lusaka and Livingstone. **Fly-drive safaris** operate into the seasonal camp in Liuwa Plain National Park. If you have your **own vehicle**, Zambia's southwest corner can be reached by driving from Livingstone to Kazungula, crossing the border to Botswana and heading north through Namibia to Katima Mulilo. This avoids the more direct, but pot holed, Zambian route and joins up with an all-weather gravel road leading to Ngonye Falls and Mongu.

On an organized safari you will have a choice of game drives, walking safaris and boat trips to explore this remote region. Independent travellers should be prepared for limited and erratic local transport and poor roads (particularly in the wet season).

Kafue National Park
LUXURY
Hippo Lodge, PO Box 31253, Maunda Road, Lusaka; tel: (261) 242083, fax: 295 398, email: hippolodge@zamnet.zm Located on the east bank of Kafue River in the northern section of the park, three two-room chalets, six-bed self-catering villa and four *en-suite* safari tents, swimming pool, walking safaris, game drives,

fishing, boat trips, excursions to Busanga Plains.
Kainga Safari Lodge, PO Box 160, Post Bag E891, Lusaka, satellite tel (17:00–19:00 GMT): +88 1 631 51 8089, email: info@kaingu-lodge.com, website: www.kaingu-lodge.com Located in southern kafue, four *en-suite* tented chalets on raised decks overlooking Kafue River, game drives, walks, fishing, river trips, specialist archaeological, birding and butterfly excursions.
Lunga River Lodge and Busanga Bush Camp, African Experience, PO Box 30106, Lusaka, satellite tel (May–Nov only): (873) 762 093 985, e-mail: safari africa@experience.co.za Lunga has a riverside position on the park's northern boundary, six thatched *en-suite* chalets, sundeck over the river, plunge pool, game drives, walks, canoeing, river cruises, fishing; Busanga is located on plains, four thatch-covered *en-suite* tents and game drives.
Mukambi Safari Lodge and Plains Camp, Post Bag E523, Lusaka, tel: (01) 292 693, website: www.mukambi.com Lodge located in southern Kafue, eight twin chalets with four-poster beds, family villa with two bedrooms and living room, five safari tents with thatched roofs, game drives, boat cruises, walking safaris. Plains Camp with three *en-suite* safari tents operates on

Busanga Plains during dry season.

Musungwa Safari Lodge and Camp site, PO Box 31808, Lusaka, tel: (01) 273 493, fax: 274 233. Large lodge with 23 chalets on the shores of Lake Itezhi-Tezhi, a swimming pool, tennis court, game-viewing, and nearby camp site with good facilities.

LUXURY/BUDGET

Lufupa Lodge, and Kafwala Rapids Camp, Busanga Trails Ltd, PO Box 37538, Lusaka, tel: (01) 214 237, email: zambia@wilderness.co.zm website: www.busangatrails.com Lufupa is at confluence of Kafue and Lufupa rivers, large lodge with 10 thatched *en-suite* rondavels, budget camp site, game drives, boat trips, walking safaris and fishing; Kafwala Rapids Camp overlooks rapids on Kafue River, three thatched *en-suite* rondavels, game drives, fishing.

Puku Pan Safari Lodge, tel: (01) 266 927, e-mail: puku pan@zamnet.zm website: www.pukupan.com Beside Kafue River, seven thatched *en-suite* cottages each with a large verandah, self-catering cottage, camp site nearby with shower and toilet, game drives, walks, boat trips and fishing.

Nchila Wildlife Reserve
MID-RANGE/BUDGET

Nchila Wildlife Reserve, PO Box 20241, Kitwe, tel: (00870) 762 642 275 (part-time satellite phone),

e-mail: nchila@nchila-wildlife-reserve.com website: www.nchila-wildlife-reserve.com Two twin and one family chalet, lounge and dining room, full board or self-catering with fully equipped kitchen, some farm food available, game drives, budget camping, 4x4 vehicle and driver for hire.

Barotseland
LUXURY

Lungwebungu Camp, operated by Royal Barotse Safaris (*see* below). Bush camp located 400km (249 miles) up the Zambezi from Mutemwa Lodge; premier spot for tiger fishing, plus other species; safaris tents, well-equipped 6m (20ft) aluminium fishing boats.

BUDGET

Lyambai Hotel, PO Box 910193, Mongu, tel: (07) 221 271. Simple hotel located near boat terminal with 17 *en-suite* rooms.

Liuwa Plain National Park
LUXURY

7nt Fly-in safari organised by Royal Barotse Safaris (*see* below) to coincide with the wildebeest migration in Nov.

Note: Royal Barotse Safaris run Maziba Bay and Mutemwa.

Ngonye Falls
LUXURY

Maziba Bay Lodge, Royal Barotse Safaris, tel: (27 11) 234 1747, fax: 234 1748, email: mutemwa.lodge@mweb.co.za website: www.mutemwa.com Reed and thatch chalets 5km (3 miles) downstream of falls, rafting, canoeing, fishing, and bird-watching.

Mutemwa Lodge, Eight luxury *en-suite* bush tents beside river, comfortable lounge, dining boma, swimming pool, canoeing, fishing, Fly-in safaris combining Maziba Bay, Mutemwa, Liuwa Plains, Barotseland and Sioma Ngwezi National Park .

TOURS AND EXCURSIONS

African Experience (*see* page 120 for contact details) can arrange two-day **canoeing safaris** on the Lunga River, camping overnight with simple bucket shower and bush toilet facilities. They also run week-long **mobile safaris** with an emphasis on either walking or canoeing. Nights are spent in fly camps, the Lunga Lodge and Busanga Bush Camp.

SENANGA	J	F	M	A	M	J	J	A	S	O	N	D
AVERAGE TEMP. °F	77	77	77	75	70	64	64	70	77	79	77	77
AVERAGE TEMP. °C	25	25	25	24	21	18	18	21	25	26	25	25
RAINFALL in	6	6	4	1	0	0	0	0	0	2	2	7
RAINFALL mm	165	155	93	26	3	0	0	1	43	61	181	

Travel Tips

Tourist Information

The Zambia National Tourist Board (ZNTB) has offices in the **United Kingdom** (London), the **USA** (New York), **South Africa** (Bruma), **Australia** (Sydney) and **Italy** (Milan). ZNTB's **Zambian head office** is at PO Box 30017, Century House, Cairo Road, Lusaka, tel: (01) 229 087, fax: 225 174, e-mail: zntb@zamnet.zm website: www.zambiatourism.com There are local tourist offices in Livingstone and Victoria Falls. The **Zambia Wildlife Authority** can be contacted at Private Bag 1, Chilanga. tel: (01) 278 524, fax: 278 244, email: zawaorg@zawa.org.zm Park entry fees are usually included in the cost of an organized safari.

Entry Requirements

Immigration rules are complicated and subject to change, so check the latest entry requirements before travelling. Details are available from Zambian High Commissions and Embassies in numerous countries (visit www.zambia embassy.org). Generally, all visitors need a visa, except citizens of Commonwealth countries – but there are exceptions. For example, UK tourists who travel on organized trips, booked overseas and in conjunction with local operators, will be issued with fee-waived visas on arrival. Check this with your travel agent. Single-entry visas are valid for three months. All visitors require valid passports and return air tickets.

Customs

Duty-free allowances are 400 cigarettes or 500g of tobacco, one-litre bottle of spirits and one-litre bottle of wine. There is no restriction on exporting normal souvenirs, such as baskets and carvings, but you will need a special permit for game trophies. Do not be tempted to buy products derived from endangered species (ivory, spotted cat skins, etc). Importing these into most countries is strictly illegal.

Health Requirements

Vaccinations for polio, tetanus, hepatitis A and meningococcal meningitis are recommended. You may be asked to show a certificate of yellow fever inoculation if arriving from an infected area. Rabies vaccination is unnecessary unless you plan to spend long periods in rural areas. Malaria is widespread in Zambia. Begin a course of antimalarial prophylaxis pills before leaving home. Medical insurance is extremely important – make sure it covers evacuation in the event of an emergency.

Getting to Zambia

Zambia can be reached by air, road, rail and boat. Lusaka is the main travel hub. Mpulungu is the only port. **By air:** British Airways has direct flights between London and Lusaka. Zambian Airways and South African Airways connect Lusaka with Johannesburg, while Kenya Airways has flights from Nairobi. Zambia's Mfuwe airport also receives international flights from Lilongwe, Malawi. International charter flights to Harare, Johannesburg, Kariba, Kasane, Lilongwe, Maun and Victoria Falls are available with Airwaves Zambia. Nationwide Airlines offers flights between Johannesburg and Livingstone. Zambian Airways, PO Box 310277, Lusaka International Airport, tel: (01) 271 230, fax: 271 054, email: reserva tions@zambianairways.com, website: www.zambianair ways.com, ticket sales offices at airport and Hotel Intercontinental.

Airwaves Zambia, book through Zambian Airways. Nationwide Airlines, Activity Centre, Sun International Resort, Livingstone, tel: (03) 323 360, fax: 324 575, email: nationwide.zamnet.zm, web-site: www.flynationwide.co.za

By road: Long-distance buses serve Lusaka from Dar es Salaam, Lilongwe, Harare and Johannesburg. Translux coaches take 9hr from Harare, 26hr from Johannesburg. Intercape Mainliner coaches link Zambia with South Africa via Windhoek. Intercape Mainliner, PO Box 618, Bellville 7535, South Africa, tel: (270 21) 380 4400, e-mail: info@intercape.co.za, website: www.intercape.co.za Translux, tel: (270 11) 774 3333, website: www.translux.co.za

Several overland participatory camping expeditions also visit Zambia: Guerba Expeditions Ltd, tel: (44) 01373 858 956, e-mail: info@guerba.co.uk Exodus, tel: (44) 20 8675 5550, e-mail: sales@exodus.co.uk, website: www.exodus.co.uk

By rail: The Tanzania–Zambia Railway (TAZARA) operates a twice-weekly express service between Dar es Salaam and Kapiri Moshi, north of Lusaka. TAZARA, PO Box 2834, Dar es Salaam, Tanzania, tel: (255 22) 286 5187, fax: 286 5334, email: acistz@afsat.com, website: www.tazara.co.tz

By boat: The *MV Liemba* runs scheduled services around Lake Tanganyika, connecting Mpulungu with Tanzania and Burundi.

Tour Agents

Travel in Zambia often involves remote safari camps, complex transfers and seasonal implica-tions. Making all arrangements directly with companies in Zambia is possible, but you may prefer to simplify the process by booking a fully inclusive and personally tailored package with an agent. In the UK, there is a plethora of safari travel companies. Expert Africa, tel: (44) 20 8232 9777, e-mail: info@expertafrica.com, website: www.expertafrica.com is renowned as the most knowledgeable on Zambia. Other reputable agents in the UK include Abercrombie & Kent, tel: (44) 1242 547 700, Safari Consultants, tel: (44) 01787 228 494, and Wildlife Worldwide, tel: (44) 0845 130 6982. In the USA, try Adventure Travel Desk, tel: (508) 653 4600; in South Africa, try Pulse Africa, tel: (27 11) 325 2290. For travel agents in Lusaka, *see* page 41.

What to Pack

Take light, loose-fitting clothing. Casual dress is fine on safari, but long trousers/skirts are more socially acceptable in towns and villages. Earthy tones are important on walking safaris in order to blend in with your surroundings – but avoid military-style clothes which might arouse suspicion with the authorities. During winter it

can get very cold at night, so take something warm to wear for early morning and evening game drives. Other essential safari items include sun hat, sunglasses, high factor sun cream, comfortable lightweight boots (for walking safaris), binoculars, camera (see panel on page 33), torch, water bottle, insect repellent, insect bite cream, simple first-aid and sewing kits, and wildlife field guides (see Good Reading, page 126). Remember not to pack too much. Most camps and lodges have same-day laundry services, while many light aircraft flights have weight restrictions of around 12kg (26lb). Pack everything in a soft holdall, not a rigid suitcase.

Money Matters

Currency: Although the offi-cial currency is kwacha (Kw), most hotels, lodges, camps, air charter companies, safari operators, etc quote prices in

---

PUBLIC HOLIDAYS

1 January • New Year's Day
12 March • Youth Day
March or **April** • Good Friday & Holy Saturday
1 May • Labour Day
25 May • Africa Freedom Day
First Monday of July • Heroes' Day
First Tuesday of July • Unity Day
First Monday of August • Farmers' Day
24 October • Independence Day
25 December • Christmas Day
26 December • Boxing Day

US$. The kwacha comes in denominations ranging from Kw50–50,000.

What to take: A mixture of traveller's cheques (in either US$ or UK£), some US$ cash and a credit card.

Exchange: Banks and *bureaux de change* in major towns and cities will exchange traveller's cheques and cash in US$ and UK£. Commission is charged. Bank opening hours vary, but most are open Mon–Fri 08:30–14:30, Sat 09:00–11:30. Avoid black market street dealers.

Credit cards: Widely accepted in the main hotels, lodges, restaurants, travel agents and shops, credit cards can also be used in some banks for cash advances. Standard Chartered and Barclays Banks have ATMs which accept Visa cards for cash advances.

Tipping: Service charges (10 per cent) are usually included, and tipping is discouraged (some even say illegal). However, for good service a 10 per cent tip is appreciated and often expected.

Taxes: Departure tax is payable in US$ cash.

Accommodation

Places to stay range from luxury 5-star hotels to budget camp sites. As a whole, Zambia has a reputation for being quite expensive and many camps and lodges aim for an upmarket, overseas market. Complicated logistics and seasonal operation are largely responsible for this – but you also get high standards of accommodation, food and service for your money. Budget hostels and camp sites are concentrated in Lusaka and Livingstone, which also have good-value public transport. Camp sites and self-catering chalets are found in several national parks, but unless you are driving your own fully equipped 4x4, you need to budget extra for travel, food supplies and activities. Reasonably priced guesthouses in larger towns are a good mid-range option.

Eating Out

International cuisine is available at major hotels and safari camps. Despite their remote location, lodges and bush camps often prepare sumptuous gourmet meals. Game meats are available at restaurants in Lusaka, Livingstone and Victoria Falls. In rural areas be sure to sample Zambia's staple dish of *nsima*. Those with more adventurous palates should try fried termites which are delicious sautéd with a pinch of salt and washed down with local Mosi or Rhino beer.

Transport

Travellers with plenty of time will see more of rural Zambia (and meet more Zambians) by travelling overland rather than flying. However, due to the large distances, remote locations and generally poor road network, most visitors use scheduled or charter flights.

Air: Airwaves Zambia has scheduled flights to Ndola, Mfuwe, Chipata, Livingstone and Lower Zambezi National Park – all designed to connect with international arrivals from London, Nairobia and Johannesburg. Proflight has direct shuttles between Lusaka, Lower Zambezi and Mfuwe, as well as regular flights connecting Lusaka, Ndola and Solwezi. Airwaves and Proflight also offer charter flights throughout Zambia, along with other air charter operators such as Avocet Air Link, Lunga Air Shuttle (to Kafue National Park) and Staravia.

Airwaves Zambia, *see* Getting to Zambia, page 122–123.

Avocet Air Link, PO Box 32056, Lusaka, tel/fax: (01) 236 437, email: avocet@zamnet.zm

Lunga Air Shuttle, *see* Lunga River Lodge, page 120.

CONVERSION CHART

FROM	TO	MULTIPLY BY
Millimetres	Inches	0.0394
Metres	Yards	1.0936
Metres	Feet	3.281
Kilometres	Miles	0.6214
Square kilometres	Square miles	0.386
Hectares	Acres	2.471
Litres	Pints	1.760
Kilograms	Pounds	2.205
Tonnes	Tons	0.984

To convert Celsius to Fahrenheit: x 9 ÷ 5 + 32

Proflight, Lusaka International Airport, tel: (01) 271 032, fax: 271 139, email: proflight@iconnect.zm, website: www.proflight-zambia.com Staravia, PO Box 34273, Lusaka, tel: (01) 291 962, website: www.staraviazambia.com

Car hire: Drive on the left in Zambia and err on the cautious side of speed limits – 100kph (62mph) may be the limit outside urban areas, but you wouldn't want to hit a pothole at this speed. An international driver's licence is required to hire a car from one of several agencies in Lusaka and major towns. Remote areas demand at least two **4x4 vehicles** (one to act as a back-up in case the other gets stuck), as well as experienced and confident 4x4 drivers. Land Rovers and Toyota Land Cruisers are available at car hire agents in Lusaka, Livingstone and Ndola.

Taxis: Useful for getting around Lusaka or for travelling between Livingstone and the Victoria Falls, taxis are numerous and have no meters – so agree on a price before setting off.

Buses: Long-distance coach services operate from the bus station on Sapele Road, Lusaka. Inexpensive local buses serve all the main towns. Faster, slightly more expensive minibuses are also available.

Trains: Lines link Lusaka to Livingstone and the Copperbelt.

Business Hours

Shops are generally open Mon–Fri 08:00–17:00, Sat 08:00–13:00.

USEFUL PHRASES

ENGLISH	BEMBA	NYANJA
hello	*shani*	*bwanji*
goodbye	*shalapo*	*pitani bwino*
how are you?	*uli shani?*	*muli bwanji?*
I am fine	*ndi bwino*	*ndili bwino*
thank you	*natotela*	*dzikomo*
yes	*eya ye*	*inde*
no	*awe*	*iyayi*
where can I find...?	*kwisa...?*	*alikuta...?*
how much?	*shinga?*	*zingati?*

Time Difference

Zambia is two hours ahead of GMT.

Communications

Zambia's postal system is fine for postcards and letters, but send valuable items by courier Telephones (usually using pay cards) are in post offices and other public buildings. To call Zambia from abroad use the international access code 260. Regional codes are 01 (Lusaka), 02 (Kitwe and Ndola), 03 (Livingstone), 04 (Mpika and Mpulungu), 05 (Kabwe and Serenje), 062 (Mfuwe) and 07 (Mongu). Internet cafés are mainly in Lusaka and Livingstone. Zambia's main daily papers are *The Times of Zambia* and *The Post*.

Electricity

The local current is 220 volts. Three-pin plugs are used similar to those in the UK.

Weights and Measures

Zambia uses the metric system.

Health Precautions

Insect bites: Taking a course of prophylaxis pills does not guarantee immunity to malaria. It is, therefore, crucial that you take precautions against being bitten by mosquitoes. Wear long-sleeved shirts, tuck trousers into socks and apply insect repellent to exposed skin early and late in the day when mosquitoes are most active. Always sleep under a mosquito net – preferably one that is impregnated with repellent in case you roll against the net while asleep. Mosquito coils and plug-in devices will also help. Another annoying insect is the tsetse fly. Although it can transmit sleeping sickness, this is a cattle disease rarely found in humans. Nevertheless, tsetse bites are painful and often swell up and itch furiously. Again, cover up and use repellent. Try to avoid wearing dark blue clothes which seem to attract the flies.

Sun and heat: On safari, you can be exposed to the fierce African sun for several hours each day. Take sensible precautions against sunburn and heat exhaustion by covering up, wearing a wide-brimmed hat, applying sunblock and drinking plenty of water.

Drinking water: Only drink water that has been purified. **HIV/AIDS:** Note that HIV/AIDS is widespread in Zambia.

Health Services

Good private hospitals are in Lusaka, Livingstone and Ndola.

Personal Safety

Children: Few, if any, camps in Zambia have fences. Wildlife is free to come and go – including potentially dangerous animals. You are perfectly safe during such visits as long as you stay calm and keep a respectful distance. Young children, however, who can be unpredictable and easily excitable, might alarm a peacefully browsing jumbo and that is when danger can arise. For this reason, camps generally have a minimum age limit of around 12 – but check beforehand. Walking safaris are particularly unsuitable for young children.

Spiders and snakes: Yes, Zambia has both! However, they will do their utmost to give you a wide berth. In fact, you would be lucky to even glimpse, say, a python. One note of caution, however. Walking safaris are wonderful for getting close to nature but don't start poking around in termite holes or dead trees. These are the kind of places snakes have gone to avoid you. Leave the detective work to your expert guide.

Adventure activities: There is an inherent risk in bungee jumping and other adrenaline activities at Victoria Falls. You will be asked to sign an indemnity waiver before undertaking them. Read it carefully and be aware of the limits of your personal travel insurance.

Petty theft: This does exist in Lusaka and major towns. Read the advice on page 32, but don't let it put you off. The vast majority of Zambians are friendly and helpful.

Emergencies

Parts of Zambia are very remote and in the event of an emergency you will need an air evacuation. All camps and lodges have radio links to facilitate this. Reputable companies will also have guides trained in wilderness first aid.

Etiquette

It is always polite to ask before photographing people.

If they refuse, smile and try to strike up a rapport with them, rather than simply shrugging and walking away. Similarly, never let your enthusiasm for getting that 'perfect shot' cause distress to wildlife. Photographing official buildings and anything military in Zambia is not advisable.

Language

Although English is the official language and is widely used, Zambia has at least 16 cultural groups speaking over 70 dialects. After English, Bemba is the next most common language, spoken mainly in rural northern Zambia. Other dialects include Lozi, spoken in Barotseland, and Tumbuka, which is used mainly in eastern regions.

GOOD READING

Alden, Estes et al (1995) *National Audubon Society Field Guide to African Wildlife* (Knopf).

Estes, Otte et al (1999) *The Safari Companion: A Guide to Watching African Mammals* (Chelsea Green Publishing Company).

Ferguson, James (1999) *Expectations of Modernity: Myths and Meanings of Urban Life on the Zambian Copperbelt* (University of California Press).

Kingdon, Jonathan (1997) *The Kingdon Field Guide to African Mammals* (Academic Press).

Lamb, Christina (2000) *The Africa House* (Penguin).

Livingstone, David (2001) *Missionary Travels in South Africa* (Narrative Press).

Livingstone, David (2004) *The Zambesi Expedition* (Kessinger Publishing).

Newman, Kenneth (2002) *Newman's Birds of Southern Africa* (New Holland).

Owens, Mark and Delia (1993) *The Eye of the Elephant: An Epic Adventure in the African Wilderness* (Mariner Books).

Reader, John (1999) *Africa: A Biography of the Continent* (Vintage).

Sinclair et al (2002) *Birds of Southern Africa* (Princeton University Press).

Stuart, Chris and Tilde (2003) *A Field Guide to the Tracks and Signs of Southern and East African Wildlife* (Struik Publishers).

INDEX

Note: Numbers in **bold**
indicate photographs